THE ART OF THE
DRAMATIST

J B Priestley

THE ART OF THE DRAMATIST

And Other Writings on Theatre

SELECTED AND INTRODUCED
BY TOM PRIESTLEY

OBERON BOOKS
LONDON

First published in this collection in 2005 by Oberon Books Ltd.
521 Caledonian Road, London N7 9RH
Tel: 020 7607 3637 / Fax: 020 7607 3629
e–mail: oberon.books@btinternet.com
www.oberonbooks.com

First publication: Individual dates for extracts given after first
instance of quotation. *Jenny Villiers* (novel), *Delight, Margin
Released, Instead of the Trees, Rain Upon Godshill, Outcries and
Asides, The Art of the Dramatist* first published by Heinemann.
The Story of Theatre first published by Rathbone (illustrated
edition). *The Arts Under Socialism* first published by Turnstile.
Theatre Outlook first published by Nicholson and Watson.

A catalogue record for this book is available from the British
Library.

ISBN: 1 84002 294 9

Printed in Great Britain by Antony Rowe Ltd, Chippenham.

'I believe now that in our life, as in the Theatre, the scenery and costumes and character make-ups and props are only a shadow show, to be packed up and put away when the performance is over. And what's real and enduring, perhaps indestructible, is all that so many fools imagine to be flimsy and fleeting – the innermost and deepest feelings – the way an honest artist sees his work – the root and heart of a real personal relationship – the flame – the flame burning clear. And Pauline, I believe that for all our vulgar mess of paint and canvas and lights and advertisement, we who work in the Theatre, just because it's a living symbol of the mystery of life, we help to guard and to show the flame. Silly as we look, my dear, we're the servants of the divine secret.'

from *Jenny Villiers*
1946 (play) and 1947 (novel)

CONTENTS

THERE IS no more enchanting box of tricks in the world than a theatre, especially a theatre that makes its own scenery and costumes. I have known quite a number of middle-aged men and women who were compelled, for one reason or another, to take an interest in one of these theatres, and then soon found themselves bewitched by it all, rejuvenated, given a whole range of new interests. I have known more than one fine group of young people who would feel as if the world were suddenly drained of all colour and fun if their theatre were taken away from them. And I have seen, with both amusement and admiration, how this playhouse work has cut right across the various social levels of the community, bringing the classes together on one common footing. You cannot stand on your dignity in this kind of work. You all start together on a new level, and come away from it feeling refreshed, as one always does when that curse of our English life – our class system – has been temporarily removed.

from *The Theatre and You*, 1938

INTRODUCTION

Tom Priestley

MY FATHER was always fascinated by the Theatre, and the magic it wove with and for its audience. We shall see how he evolved a theory of how this exactly functioned, which he called Dramatic Experience; this he differentiated from the vicarious pleasure of Show Business, which never engages the total mind and imagination of the spectator, but just involves a mindless curiosity and amusement. But while he believed firmly in what he calls 'Serious Theatre', he insisted on the importance of entertainment to leaven the solemnity.

Once he entered the Theatre in the early 1930s, he immersed himself in it, and was soon able to analyse its problems and to suggest solutions. Theatrical historians will be able to judge how far these suggestions were instrumental in changing the way the Theatre was organised after the Second World War, but it seems to me that many of the problems still persist to this day. Possibly some of his solutions were too radical and hence impractical, but they were always based on his love of the Theatre, and his profound feeling of the vital importance of the Theatre for a healthy nation; healthy in mind and spirit, in the world of the imagination, and healthy in the sense of community, growing from the audience itself, a group of people welded together by common experience, sharing for that moment the 'pity and fear' of the drama.

He believed also in the continuity of the Theatre, just as he did in the continuity of Literature; both evolving from the past and growing towards the future. The past irradiating the present, and the present the future. He insisted too on the changeability of convention. Each convention is good for its particular age. As time passes, it loses its vitality, and needs constantly refreshing by change and evolution. No convention is better than another; it merely expresses a reaction to the past. The pendulum constantly swings to and fro.

The first two volumes of the Oberon collection of J B Priestley's Theatre presented, in each case, three plays – comedies in *Plays One*, dramas in *Plays Two* – with an introduction examining the background, content and circumstances of production.

Now we move to a different area, going, as it were, behind the scenes, out of the auditorium, away from the plush seats, the programmes, the interval drinks, to a world of offices, auditions, rehearsal rooms and workshops; somewhere between the closing pages of the script and the curtain rising on the performance, incorporating casting, publicity, invest-ment, audience figures and reviews. All of these my father mastered, because, as we shall see, he did far more than deliver the text and retire to his typewriter.

He was blessed with tireless creative energy. Glancing through Alan Day's authoritative bibliography I find 13 plays published between 1932 and 1939, a single one-act play and 11 full-length plays in the 1940s, five one-act and six full-length plays in the 1950s (including *Dragon's Mouth* and *The White Countess* co-written with Jacquetta Hawkes – the latter performed but never published) and in 1964 his masterly adaptation of Iris Murdoch's *A Severed Head*. Add to that his collaboration on the dramatisation of *The Good Compan-ions* which opened in 1931, and it adds up to 32 full-length plays and six one-act plays – an impressive total; many of them produced by his own management company. He also directed at least two: *Ever Since Paradise* and *Dragon's Mouth*.* In the 1930s alone he wrote at least five novels,

* Professor Holger Klein in his 1988 book *J B Priestley's Plays* lists 38 published plays and a further 31 unpublished and never performed in the theatre though some were adapted for radio or television, or even reworked as fiction.

three major works of non-fiction, several filmscripts, and over 450 articles, as well as 14 full-length plays. He admitted himself that he had probably written too much in his long career, and might have done better to concentrate on one single aspect of his writing and that would have been the Theatre, for which he felt he had a greater natural affinity than for fiction.

In this anthology we follow three strands: first the background to his interest in and love of the Theatre, a kind of theatrical autobiography, told in his own words; secondly his overall view of the History of Theatre up to his day, which gives his view of the path leading from the past to the present of his time; and thirdly his attitude towards the Theatre once he had begun working in it – his views on the weaknesses of the system and his suggestions for their improvement, as well as a profound analysis of the very experience of Theatre-going for any audience.

Interlaced with these are a few articles on aspects of his experience working in the Theatre, and finally notes on his method of writing and advice to young playwrights.

I have occasionally included a note of explanation (in italics), or a short comment to link passages together, but have kept these to a minimum. For an anthology of a prolific writer, it seems wiser to stand aside and let him tell his story.

Thanks

I would particularly like to thank James Hogan for his encouragement and patience, a rare publisher of the Old School, and Dan Steward for his insightful editing; thanks also to my great-nephew Toby Goaman Dodson, JBP's great grandson, who helped enormously with research and with taming my laptop; thanks to Tony Yablon for permission to reproduce the 1938 letter to Arthur Berry; and to Michael Nelson of the J B Priestley Society for his useful suggestions; and to Alison Cullingford and John Brooker of the J B Priestley Archive at the J B Priestley Library in the University of Bradford; and to Nicki Stoddart of Peters, Fraser and Dunlop, a staunch ally; and to Alan Day for his masterly bibliography.

TP, 2005

THE MAKING OF A DRAMATIST

WHEN I WAS a lad and regularly took my place in the queue for the early doors of the gallery in the old Theatre Royal, Bradford, the actors on their way to the stage door had to walk past us. I observed them with delight. In those days actors looked like actors and like nothing else on earth. There was no mistaking them for wool merchants, shipping clerks, and deacons of Baptist chapels, all those familiar figures of my boyhood. They wore suits of startling check pattern, outrageous ties, and preposterous overcoats reaching down to their ankles. They never seemed to remove all their make-up as actors do now, and always had a rim of blue-black round their eyelids. They did not belong to our world and never for a moment pretended to belong to it. They swept past us, fantastically overcoated, with trilbies perched raffishly on brilliantined curls, talking of incredible matters in high tones, merely casting a few sparkling glances – all the more sparkling because of that blue-black – in our direction; and then vanished through the stage door, to reappear, but out of all recognition, in the wigs and knee-breeches of David Garrick or The Only Way. And my young heart, as innocent as an egg, went out to these romantic beings; and perhaps it was then, although I have no recollection of it, that the desire was born in me to write one day for the Theatre.

Delight 45, 1949, Seeing the Actors

J B Priestley was born on 13 September 1894 in Bradford in the West Riding of Yorkshire. Bradford then was a wealthy town – the world centre of the wool trade – and so combined a hearty provincialism with a cosmopolitanism fostered by the international nature of the trade. There was a healthy appetite for the arts and the funds to promote them. Remember that in those days there was no radio, television or

cinema (films started off as a turn in the Music Hall, called the Bioscope).
It was a great time for home entertainment – songs round the piano
and, a family favourite, charades.

Our favourite scene at home when I was a boy was the Fat
Men Scene, which had to be brought in somehow, as even I,
with my sterner standard of the game, admitted; and indeed I
would not have allowed it to be overlooked. My father and
some of his friends needed only a few cushions to be
magnificent Fat Men, while I and my like took to pillows and
overcoats, and blew out our cheeks until we dissolved, as we
always did very soon, into laughter. The antics were simple
indeed, and followed a familiar recipe; but all of us, even the
stateliest wives of deacons, laughed till we cried. And now,
40 years afterwards, I am a Fat Man, without the help of a
single cushion; and every night, on 20 stages, in places I have
never seen, they play my charades.

Delight 23, Charades

But Bradford was also well endowed with theatres, as he told me in
our conversation for my film Time and the Priestleys:

We had two theatres: the Prince's played mostly melodramas
in repertory, but the other theatre, the Theatre Royal, was a
first class date for touring companies, a very nice theatre too,
not very big but very good. We had two music halls: the Moss
& Stoll and the Palace which was underneath the Prince's
Theatre. I went to both; I went to everything.

In his teens when he was already working in a wool office and writing
in his spare time, and he found an unpaid job writing a column for a
local Labour weekly, the Bradford Pioneer; *this undoubtedly gave*
him the opportunity to go regularly to both Theatre and music hall.

I was a constant and enthusiastic playgoer, defying the heat and discomfort of those old galleries. I enjoyed almost everything, from *Oedipus Rex* and *The Trojan Women* to *The Waltz Dream* and *The Count of Luxemburg and The Merry Widow*, of course, though, for some reason I have forgotten now, it was never one of my favourite Viennese operettas, all of which, incidentally, had real scores and orchestras, not just night club noise. I cannot say I enjoyed everything; I had reservations about a certain type of gentlemanly melodrama then in vogue; I remember one called *A White Man*. Appearing at the Theatre Royal, between Benson's Shakespeare and Edward Compton's Sheridan and Goldsmith, these pieces seemed contrived and anaemic, inferior to the full-blooded melodrama we had every week at the other Theatre, the Prince's – *A Royal Divorce*, *The Face at the Window*, and the like. Yes, in my teens I could be said to be stage-struck, and it was an advantage to me long afterwards, when I came to work in the Theatre, that I had left this complaint far behind, like the measles and mumps of my childhood.

Margin Released, 1962

If and when I was ignoring the Theatre Royal I was probably going to the Empire, a fine music hall. These were the great days of the halls, which offered us more talent in a month than the BBC and ITV can scrape up in a year. I have tried – and not without success, I think – to reproduce the atmosphere and flavour of those music halls in a novel called *Lost Empires*. However, I must add that at that time I knew nothing about how variety worked, had never in fact been behind the scenes.

We had then in Bradford a Playgoers' Society, which often gave readings of Shaw and other heavyweights. There is a lot to be said for readings of this kind, in which no attempt at production is made but you are given the characters and the lines. Intelligent amateurs often read well but are stiff and awkward in a production, so it is better to let them do play readings, with the characters sitting in a long line but standing up when they are supposed to be in the scene.

Guardian, 5 April 1974

Bradford was a lively though rather grim place, redeemed by wonderful countryside within easy reach. Similarly the ordinariness of everyday life was redeemed by the magic (his favourite word) of the interior world of the imagination, available in Literature and the Theatre. The feeling of mystery, of otherness, is one of the enduring themes of his work. This surely was part of the attraction of the Theatre; it was a window into another world.

The Theatre itself, however, was much further removed from me then than it is from a teenager now. Except for that foreshortened but brilliant view we had from the gallery, it belonged to another world, closed to us. The gallery queue, where I waited many a freezing hour, used to extend towards the stage door, so that I often saw the actors making their way there. More than twenty years later, I sketched a portrait of one of them, Charlie Appleby in *Eden End*, but not out of any contemporary experience of him and his kind. The actors then were almost visitors from outer space. I could not imagine them in their digs, drinking bottled beer and eating ham and eggs. Actresses, wickedly painted even off the stage, were even more remote, hardly related biologically to the women and girls one knew, belonging to other orders of being, fays and sylphs and hamadryads. The whole business and interior traffic of the Theatre were unimaginable then; managements and agents and contracts, runs in the West End, bookings for Number One and Number Two tours, authors' royalties of five, seven-and-a-half, ten per cent of the gross, all were beyond the reach of knowledge, not even to be imagined. Is it surprising then that although I was a playgoer I never even thought of attempting a play?

Margin Released

When the First World War began, he soon volunteered and spent five dreadful years in the army enduring the horrors of the trenches. On demobilisation in 1919 he went up to Cambridge on an officer's grant, took his degree in two years, married and started earning his living by writing.

The period 1919–24 covers the time when I was up at Cambridge and then left it to freelance in London. I would take a day ticket from Cambridge to London, attend a matinee, then an evening performance, and get the late train back. Many of the galleries in those days were terrible. You were so high you were hardly inside the theatre; you sat on wooden benches about six inches wide; and all you saw of the actors were the tops of their heads. My most memorable experience came at the end of this period, in 1924, when Fagan brought his production of *The Cherry Orchard* from Oxford to the Royalty Theatre. It was 'all a wonder and a wild desire'.

Guardian, 5 April 1974

Good theatre seats were comparatively dear then, so if we could not find somebody, a dramatic critic or friendly editor, to give us complimentary tickets, we went to the pit or gallery. I remember paying about ninepence or so at the old Alhambra to see the most astonishing galaxy of prima ballerinas that ever blazed on one stage. And the Lyric, Hammersmith was cheap enough, and there Nigel Playfair's production of *The Beggar's Opera* was running. We knew every word and note of it, used to roar them out round the piano, but still returned, time after time, to the Lyric. It seemed to me then – and after a quarter of a century of work in the Theatre, I am not prepared to change my mind – an enchanting production, the best in its kind we have ever had in this country, never beaten by later attempts to get away from Playfair's style, Lovat Fraser's décor, Frederick Austin's modest but rather luscious arrangement of the music. On the other hand, although I saw the production, I was never an enthusiastic admirer of the other long run, *The Immortal Hour*, at another old theatre brought out of shabbiness and neglect, the Regent, near King's Cross. But if you wanted perfection of a very different theatrical style, extreme naturalism, there were the productions of Galsworthy's plays by Basil Dean at the St Martin's, where so many good actors learnt their trade. You might dislike this kind of play, this method of production, yet you could not deny Dean the triumph of his formidable qualities, which we are beginning to miss in the Theatre. There was also some good new work being done up at the Everyman Theatre, Hampstead, by Norman Macdermott. And Gerald du Maurier, who as actor-manager had every virtue except the courage necessary for experiment, was still at Wyndham's. I was told not long ago, by way of a rebuke, that our London post-war Theatre might no longer be creative but that it has reached greatness in its interpretation; but it seems to me – and I speak of one of my own trades – that outside Shakespeare both the production and the acting in the 1920s were generally superior to ours. But then the economics of the Theatre were much sounder. It had hardly begun to have colossal rivals that drew on its talent without making any adequate return for their loans and raids.

The music-hall of today is nothing but the ghost of what it was in the early 1920s in London. It had already passed its peak even then, but some of the ripe old turns were still with us. You could look in at the Coliseum, as I often did on a winter afternoon, and see Little Tich and Harry Tate, and there were still some glorious drolls at the Holborn Empire (a sad loss; it had a fine thick atmosphere of its own), the Victoria Palace and the rest. There were no microphones and nobody needed them. There were no stars who had arrived by way of amusing farmers' wives and invalids on the radio. There were no reputations that had been created by American gramophone records for teenagers. The men and the women who topped the bills had spent years getting there, learning how to perfect their acts and to handle their audiences. Of course there was plenty of vulgar rubbish, but all but the very worst of it had at least some zest and vitality. And the audiences, which laughed at jokes and did not solemnly applaud them as BBC audiences do now, were an essential part of the show, they too had vitality, and were still close to the Cockneys who helped to create, a generation earlier, the English music-hall of the great period, the folk art out of which, among other things, came the slapstick of the silent films, especially those of Chaplin.

'Coming to London', *London Magazine*, February 1956

From about the middle of the 1920s I did little Theatre-going. I was living well out of London, hard at work on books.

Guardian, 5 April 1974

Hard at work indeed. Between 1923 and 1929 he produced 15 books, of which five were reprints of essays published elsewhere. The fifteenth was his bestseller The Good Companions, *not his own favourite novel but certainly his most successful. This was followed in 1930 by* Angel Pavement, *another success; now at last the pressure was off him to produce book after book and he could turn from Literature to the Theatre.*

We can catch a glimpse of what he felt and thought about the Theatre, before he himself entered it professionally, from an article he wrote in 1930, 'I Look at the Theatre', with the topical byline, By J B Priestly [sic] (Novelist, author of The Good Companions):

I do not pretend to be a serious student of the Theatre – my main interests are elsewhere – but I have been a steady playgoer ever since I was a schoolboy. I like the atmosphere of the playhouse, especially when the playhouse admits to a certain artificial gaiety and is rather pretty and absurd in gilt and coloured lights. Those bleak modern theatre interiors, suggesting a place for scientific lectures, repel me, and I believe that behind their austerities there is a mistaken idea of the Theatre. The basis of the Theatre is entertainment. Thus, a performance of *Hamlet* is superb entertainment; it may be many other things too, but first and foremost it is superb entertainment.

This does not mean that the Theatre cannot be serious. I do not really prefer farces and revues to tragedies or what for want of a better name we must call 'serious plays', but nevertheless I find myself going to see farces and revues far more often, for I certainly prefer a good farce or revue to a bad tragedy or serious play.

[...]

The modern Theatre became entirely serious for me, something that could conjure beauty out of life, when I sat through my first performance of *The Cherry Orchard*. Here, in this strange play about a group of idle and fantastic Russians, the thing was done. Here was life in all its abundance and richness, its pathos and humour, its terror and beauty. Throughout this play, you feel you are in a definite place that exists somewhere, and not in some vague generalized Theatre scene.

Most modern plays do not satisfy me, even though they may possibly entertain me for an hour or so, just because they have in them little sense of character and atmosphere. They are an affair of puppets moving in a vacuum. The situations in which their characters find themselves may be dramatic enough, but if these characters seem to you people made of cardboard, creatures who had no existence before the play began and will have none when it is over, it is difficult to take such situations very seriously.

I want to come out of the theatre, not feeling that I have been hocus-pocussed into being emotional for an hour about something that will be gone like smoke from my mind the next day, but feeling that I have just been given a great chunk of experience and that my memory has been correspondingly enriched.

Time after time, I have read notices of plays that were blamed because 'nothing happened' in some particular act, and I have seen the play afterwards and discovered that those acts were easily the most satisfying, just because they gave me a rich sense of life. I have no objection to plays that are crammed with action and strong situations; they are melodrama; and melodrama can be great fun. It does not belong to the serious Theatre, however. And it is not debates on questions of the day, not is it symbolism or producer's antics, that will make the serious Theatre entirely serious and satisfying. It is character and atmosphere.

Theatre Arts Monthly, August 1930

He collaborated on the stage version of The Good Companions *and no doubt tried his hand at playwriting on his own, but to no avail – before producing his first solo play,* Dangerous Corner, *which plunged him into the world of the Theatre.*

It was in May 1932 that I arrived in the London Theatre. The play was *Dangerous Corner*. It was brilliantly directed by Tyrone Guthrie, who introduced many new devices that are now commonplaces of production, and, though it had no star part, Flora Robson's performance dominated it. The irony department had followed me through the stage door. The play itself was a trick thing, in which time divided at the sound of a musical cigarette-box. I wrote it in a week, chiefly to prove that a man might produce long novels and yet be able to write effectively, using the strictest economy, for the stage. It was so poorly received by the daily press – 'This is Mr Priestley's first play and we don't mind if it is also his last'; that kind of welcome – that there was talk on the Saturday of taking it off, after five performances. If it had been taken off that night, I doubt if the play would ever have been heard of again. But with more favourable Sunday notices, especially from James Agate and Ivor Brown, it had a comfortable run, and six years later it was revived... I kept away from the Theatre until I knew my children's food and clothing could be paid for, and it was out of a desire to escape the worst effects, once I was working in the Theatre, that I formed my own production company. This took me into the thick of it, but for some years I enjoyed being there, working on the production side with friends like Irene Hentschel and Basil Dean and Michael MacOwan, and on the managerial side with other friends like A D Peters, J P Mitchelhill and Thane Parker. Working in the Theatre with people is tricky, especially if you are the author as well, because in there, away from daylight and common sense, everybody knows best. Not being really sure of anything, we all pretend to be absolutely certain about everything. So friendship, as distinct from the false good-fellowship that comes and goes so quickly, prevents colleagues from turning into so many irritants...

Shaw did not approve of my production company. (I must add here that with one enterprise or another I did help some other dramatists to reach the public.) At that time Shaw was declaring that any manager who revived his plays at cheap prices would make a fortune. He had only to make a telephone call or two and then find his cheque-book to begin testing the truth of this assertion, but he never did. He told me – more than once, I think – that management would ruin me; it was a short cut to bankruptcy. He was quite wrong.

Margin Released

When he was young he even had ambitions as a performer. In our filmed conversation I had asked him if he did any performing, and he told me: 'A little – yes. I had thoughts in that direction. I remember I appeared several times at the Mechanics Institute, which offered entertainment, but not of the highest!'

Once I had to do some acting of a sort in the West End, for about ten performances. This was not a publicity stunt but an attempt to save a farcical comedy, *When We Are Married*, that had just opened and finally had a long run. Frank Pettingell, who played the comic lead, a drunken West Riding photographer, was injured in a motor accident, so Basil Dean, a man not easily denied, rushed me on as a drunken West Riding photographer, at least a part not obviously beyond my physical and mental range, no Hamlet or Romeo. I cannot say if I was a good or bad actor, but I certainly knew my own lines, never fluffed or 'dried', and duly got my laughs. I didn't enjoy the experience. I seemed to be always waiting for a climax, a moment of truth and glory, that never arrived. Probably because I was not really an actor, I found it all curiously elusive, frustrating, unrewarding. And to paint one's face after an early lunch, all for the benefit of matinee audiences, waiting for the tea they had ordered, was horrible. Perhaps it was then that I began to dislike audiences, enjoying rehearsals of my plays but avoiding performances of them. In London especially, people giggle and guffaw too easily; they visit a theatre to be tickled. I always preferred if possible to open plays in the North, where they sat with tightened lips and narrowed eyes, grimly awaiting their money's worth.

Margin Released

After two and a half years as a dramatist-manager, he was co-director of the Duchess Theatre, in his words 'perhaps the prettiest intimate theatre in London', and 'fortunate to have been, so far, more successful than I expected'. On a visit to New York he reflected on the Theatre as he knew it then:

I broke into the Theatre after establishing a reputation for other kinds of work, which was not altogether an advantage but which gave me a certain perspective and detachment.

The commercial theatrical manager is often criticised as being a mere box-office hound, a pander to fashionable silliness of all kinds. This is true of some managers, though quite a few of them are ready to risk a good deal on work they like but that may have no appeal to the big public. My first criticism – and the one that chiefly influenced me when I decided to become my own manager of the Theatrical world – is that it is a terrible waster of one's time and energy. Getting a play out in the ordinary way is like trying to play croquet in Alice's Wonderland, where, if you remember, the hoops would walk away, the balls would disappear, and the live mallets wriggled all the time. That is what happens in the theatrical world. You never know where you are.

If book publishers were as chaotic as most theatrical managers the book trade would be a bedlam in a few months. I admit that it is much more difficult producing plays than it is publishing books, but, nevertheless, the business has been needlessly complicated. When I write a play – as long as the people whose judgement I trust are satisfied about it – I want to feel that there is a theatre and stage of the right size waiting for it, that the right players are there ready to interpret it. I do not want to feel – as most dramatists are compelled to feel – that now the play is written the real labour and torment are just beginning, that months of lunatic negotiating are ahead of me.

The trouble is that with a few exceptions the author is still traditionally in the Theatre a person of small consequence – that shabby little fellow who sits at the back during rehearsals, somebody of about the same importance as the second leading lady's husband. Yet the fact remains that there are two – and two only – really important people in the Theatre: the author who writes the words and the player who speaks them.

A dramatist of promise deserves the interest and affectionate encouragement of everybody who loves the Theatre. If he writes a poor play, he should be told so. The greatest dramatists in the world's history have written poor plays now and again. An artist must be allowed to experiment, to take a chance. After all it is not easy to write a good play. The Theatre as a vital modern institution cannot exist without a supply of good new plays.

New York Times, 16 December 1934

Theatre activities were disrupted by the outbreak of war in 1939; my father's energies were diverted to what he saw as his contribution to the war effort, largely his broadcasts, the famous 'Postscripts', and the less known but more frequent overseas broadcasts.

It was only in 1943 that he could turn his mind to the post-war Theatre, as we have seen in 'Future of the Theatre' (see p 73). The same year saw the production of his strongest wartime play They Came to a City, *and in 1944 a play* Desert Highway *which he wrote for and gave to the Army. That year he wrote what has turned out to be his most successful play* An Inspector Calls *which was first produced in Russia in 1945 as there was no London theatre available. My parents saw it there on a prolonged visit to Russia in the autumn of 1945. It opened in London in October 1946. There followed a busy period for J B Priestley in the Theatre. In 1947 he was chosen to be Britain's delegate for the Arts to UNESCO; his play* The Linden Tree *opened in London; sadly neglected since, it had the best first London run of any of his plays, 422 performances; he gave a lecture to the*

Fabian Society, later published as a pamphlet, 'The Arts Under Socialism' (see p 91); he also published 'Theatre Outlook', extracts from which appear later (p 130). He had a busy time in, and out of, the Theatre.

I enjoyed working in the Theatre but never saw it, as so many people did then, as a glittering playground. In the terms of that time, I was a bad Theatre man. I never attended first nights nor rushed backstage to tell actresses they had been wonderful. I disliked the West End Theatre in its glamour-gossip-column aspect. Though often successful, I was never a fashionable playwright. So far as I appealed to any particular class, I would say this was the professional middle class. (This possibly explains why I was so widely and often produced abroad, where Theatre-going tended to be more serious – not so much a party-night-out affair as it was in the West End.) Again I never cultivated the friendly acquaintance of star players, managers, critics – excluding the few who were my friends anyhow.

Guardian, 5 April 1974

Maybe a bad 'Theatre man', but he was certainly dedicated to the Theatre, and was always looking for ways in which it could be improved structurally, better organised for actors and audiences so as to provide the richest experience at a reasonable cost. He summed up his time in the Theatre in 1977 just seven years before his death:

As a highly professional dramatist, with plays going all over the world, I have had a curious relationship with the Theatre. It might be said that I have seen both more and less of it than most professional dramatists. More of it because when actually working in the Theatre I have not been confined to the role of author but have played several other roles, as a director of two producing companies. I have seen less of it because, unlike many of my colleagues, when not actually working in the Theatre I keep away from it, being busy with other things. I can think of some people I have known who never seemed to get away from the Theatre, who ate it, drank it, breathed it, almost as if they never saw daylight. This has some professional advantages, bringing with it an expertise and a sense of theatrical fashion, but it lacks the nourishment to be had in the world outside the Theatre; if my plays have travelled far – as indeed they have – it may be that the best of them have gained from this nourishment, have brought something of the world outside on to the stage, have not been too theatrically theatrical.

Wondering what was happening abroad, I have just gone through my play agent's financial statements for the last few months. The result surprised me. Money has come in from Australia, Belgium, Czechoslovakia, France, Germany, Holland, Italy, Japan, New Zealand, Scandinavia, Spain and the USA. Now there is no new dramatic material here. It is entirely a question of theatrical or TV performances of plays written thirty to forty years ago. And what conclusion can I come to here? That I am already a classic? Perhaps not; but surely that I am at least halfway there, though I doubt if there are many people here in England who would put forward even that claim for me. This is the trouble about not being an out-and-out thorough-going Theatre man, just popping into it to do some work and then popping out again to take a look at the world. I am paying for some dubiety and detachment. But a freedom from fuss and silliness is well worth the price demanded. Or isn't it, remembering that my old love for the Theatre, an essential part of my youth, hasn't entirely vanished yet?

Instead of the Trees, 1977

THE STORY OF THEATRE

Magic and Tragedy

MEN MUST have been performing long before history began. Primitive men believed in what we now call 'sympathetic magic' – the idea that if you act something you can make it happen. A hunting tribe running short of meat might decide to act the discovery and killing of a deer. If so, somebody had to pretend to be the deer, and others pretend to be the successful hunters. In its own fashion, this is as much a performance as a production of *Hamlet*.

As religions developed, the public rites connected with them involved some elements of production, acting, performance. Long before Athens became a city-state and the home of a magnificent civilisation, the Greeks had made use of choral hymns and dances in their worship; and during seasonal fertility rites had enjoyed revels and masquerades in which the performers pretended to be birds and other animals. It is generally held that we can discover in hymns and dances the origin of Greek Tragedy, and in revels and masquerades the origin of Greek Comedy.

Although theatres grew up everywhere in Greece, it is to Athens at its height during the fifth century BC that we owe the complete development of the Theatre and one of the greatest dramatic styles the world has known. It was a completely communal art: performed not for private amusement but at great public festivals, where the most important dramatic poets competed for civic prizes.

Although this classical Greek drama was true drama, its general style and atmosphere might suggest to us a kind of solemn opera rather than a play. Both tragedy and comedy were originally formal and conventional, following strict rules broken later by dramatists of genius. Both included music and dancing. Both employed a Chorus which, in tragedy, spoke with the voice of the community, expressing common points of view.

Tragic dramatists did not invent stories and characters. Their dramas were based on myths and legends familiar to everybody. Suspense and surprise were absent from this Theatre, but in terms of high poetic tragedy this was an advantage. The poets could concentrate upon giving their own interpretation of familiar stories. Since everybody knew what must happen, the poets could make use of dramatic irony; could show a proud man who thinks himself master of his fate, moving inevitably to the doom which the audience knows awaits him.

Unlike later dramas, which could be printed and so endlessly duplicated, ancient Greek dramas only existed as fragile manuscripts. Far more of them have disappeared than have survived. But the surviving dramas, coming to us almost miraculously after centuries of war, invasion, revolution, show us what a height Greek tragedy suddenly achieved. Tradition has it that the poet Thespis of Athens first used an actor as well as a chorus-leader, and this has brought him his own immortality for whatever concerns acting has since been called by the name 'Thespian'.

The first of the three great Greek tragic masters, Aeschylus (525–456 BC), introduced a second actor, which really made drama as we understand it possible. He was also celebrated for his startling effects, such as the tremendous entrance of Agamemnon in a chariot.

The second of these great tragic poets, Sophocles (c 496–06 BC), was less of an innovator, but he introduced a third actor, made less use of the chorus, and is said to have been the first dramatist to insist upon painted scenery.

The third, Euripides (c 484–06 BC) made still less use of chorus, but greatly increased the number of characters in his plays. (There are as many as eleven in *The Phoenician Women*.)

Greek scholars down the centuries have varied considerably in their estimates of Aeschylus, Sophocles and Euripides according to their own temperaments and outlook. Here we must look at them very broadly from the standpoint of world Theatre. Aeschylus was the grand originator, the first great dramatist known to us; and considered simply as a tragic poet, must be held to be the greatest. His wonderful trilogy – a group of three plays – the *Oresteia*, which shows how one crime breeds another in the doomed family of Atreus until at last civic justice (civilisation) is achieved, is a towering masterpiece of dramatic force and lofty imagination.

Regarded simply as a dramatist, Sophocles is the greatest of the three. Of all these tragedies, his *Oedipus Rex* has been played most frequently in our own Theatre. It is a short play: a marvel of tense, terse writing, and terrible dramatic irony, as within two hours the ill-fated Oedipus makes one appalling discovery after another about himself, and is changed from a king to an outcast.

Opinions differ widely about Euripides. Admirers of Sophocles and Aeschylus think him inferior and see in his work the ruin of the classical tradition. Other critics put him first because he is better at describing individual people, gives more scope for acting, is more romantic in feeling, altogether less bound by classical rules and more like a modern writer. Indeed it is hard to believe Euripides was a contemporary of Sophocles. The main idea in the older and more strictly classical Greek plays is the relation between man and the powers of the universe. In the plays of Euripides this is being replaced by the relation between one man and another, and by the idea, familiar in modern drama, that character shapes destiny.

Greek comedy took longer to develop than Greek tragedy and had no place in civic festivals for half a century. This is easy to understand. The Old Comedy – quite different from the later New Comedy – combined so many elements, choral, miming, dialogue, clowning, that only a writer of genius could fuse them successfully into drama worth a place beside the work of the tragic poets.

This genius was Aristophanes, and though his plays are rarely produced today, he must be included in any list of the world's great comic writers. His plays are too fantastic, too much 'of their time' to have had much direct dramatic influence, but many later comic writers, especially between 1500–1750, studied his work to their advantage, borrowing and adapting many of his droll ideas. He often chose a theme enabling him to use a 'masquerade' chorus as in his *Wasps*, *Birds*, *Frogs*; and introduced topical allusions and jokes, with savage, though very funny, skits on well-known characters like Euripides and Socrates.

The nearest thing we have to the Aristophanic Old Comedy is the satirical show, filled with rude remarks about people known to the audience, put together by students as an end-of-term 'rag'.

In his later plays, sometimes called Middle Comedy, Aristophanes is less fantastic and savage, cuts down the part played by the chorus to make room for more plot and acting. The contemporary interest of the drama may be judged by the fact that in *The Frogs*, Aeschylus and Euripides are competing in Hades for the privilege of returning to Athens to revive the declining art of tragedy.

The New Comedy was at its height about a hundred years later. Unfortunately only fragments of its plays survive. There is however enough of Menander, its most important dramatist, to show us what kind of drama it was. Unlike the Old Comedy – fantastic, topical, local – the New Comedy is not peculiar to a time and place, reduces the chorus to a little singing and dancing between the scenes or acts, and deals with situations and types of character that were to make their appearance over and over again, starting with the Roman dramas of Plautus and Terence. Menander and his fellow dramatists created the comedy of intrigue, character, manners that became popular in the 17th and 18th centuries and has persisted, with some changes of style, right down to the present day.

The rich and tyrannical old man, the wild young man who can be tamed by the right girl, the devoted nuisance of a servant – these and other familiar types were making their first appearance on the stage 2,250 years ago in Athens. The 'new comedy' advertised to appear next week, with its elegant witty dialogue, its impudent intrigues, its amusing clash of characters, descends directly down the ages from this New Comedy of ancient Greece.

The Romans built magnificent theatres. Unlike the Greeks who used only natural hill-sites they could raise their theatres and amphitheatres anywhere because of their skill in erecting vaults which would support rising tiers of seats and galleries.

During the Republic, Roman imitations of the New Comedy of Athens held the stage for many years and gave Terence and Plautus their reputations. But under the Empire the Theatre declined very sharply. Men of letters like Seneca amused themselves writing plays – but plays which they intended to be read and not performed.

The Roman Theatre was now no place for a dignified man of letters. It was simply part of the local amusements – on no higher level than wrestling, combats between gladiators and wild-animal shows. Actors, though often highly-paid popular figures – were not reputable citizens. Meaningless spectacles, scenes of violence, buffoonery and obscenity found their way into these shows to amuse the jaded aristocrats and Roman mobs.

When Christianity spread so widely – making many enthusiastic converts – the Theatre was merely an obscene shadow of itself. Christians were strictly forbidden to attend it – and when finally the Church had the necessary power, it excommunicated the actors and began closing the theatres.

Traces of this first bad relationship between Christianity and the Theatre lingered on. Millions of people to this day imagine that the Theatre, which was of course actually religious in its roots, is profoundly irreligious.

But one development of this decadent Roman Theatre is worth mentioning. Throughout the provinces there were wandering troupes, generally consisting of slaves owned by the master of the troupe – who would set up their little platforms and curtains and play a number of short scenes, sometimes in mime or dumb show (especially when the players could not speak the local language), sometimes improvising rough dialogue and topical jokes. The players were often acrobats, tumblers, dancers – as well as actors of a sort.

After the theatres were closed, little troupes of players still went on their travels; and it is more than likely that some never stopped performing throughout the Dark Ages when the Theatre was forgotten. After a thousand years or so, what had once been the magnificent Attic drama – with its civic festivals, tragedies and comedies that are among the notable achievements of the human mind, the Theatre had dwindled to a few carts and platforms and humble troupes of clowns and acrobats. But something was kept alive, however degraded its outer appearance. There were still performers and audiences. Men still made other men stare and laugh and wonder by some skill, however rudimentary, in the ancient art of acting.

Mystery and *Macbeth*

Throughout western Europe during the later Middle Ages the drama slowly came to life again, at first by way of the Church. In the cathedrals and larger churches it became customary at Easter and Christmas to include in the special services a few brief scenes, played by priests, illustrating the birth and death of Jesus. These drew such crowds that more elaborate versions of them began to be played outside, generally on and around the steps.

Finally the Church refused to allow priests to take part in these outside performances, which were taken over by laymen. These lay performers might belong to special companies organised for the purpose, as in France, or, as in England, to the trade guilds, which were responsible for producing various Mystery plays (after ministerium service) at festival times.

Both the plays, though still crude when considered as drama, and their staging became more and more elaborate. In southern Europe old Roman theatres were used, wooden seats were built, rough-and-ready stage machinery was contrived, and the fires and torments of Hell awaiting the wicked personages of the drama were suggested by various stage effects. In England the guilds staged productions in a different way, important because it led to the Elizabethan Theatre – the setting for Shakespeare's plays. English guilds used great wagons on which small wooden sets were built; these wagons served both as backgrounds and upper stages, with the ground in front as the lower stage. Their Mysteries too were less solemn, more popular in style than those of France, and characters like the Devil and Herod were often turned into comics.

Following the Mystery came the Morality, religious in feeling but dramatising good and bad qualities and their effect upon ordinary men. The most famous Morality, which is still often played both in theatres and out of doors, was Everyman.

We leave the Middle Ages for the Renaissance, with its new sense of discovery, freedom and adventure, its passionate interest in the classical life and literature of ancient Greece and Rome, its growing wealth and cities with their opulent way of life. Italy, filled with artists and scholars, ruled by cultured princes and dukes, led western Europe on the way towards our secular modern Theatre.

Italy led the way into the Renaissance, but soon the wealthiest power was Spain, with the gold of its American colonies at its command. Religious plays called autos, performed in Spain long before the Renaissance, continued to be performed long after it. But by the early 16th century, many Spanish writers came under Italian influence and produced both comedies of manners and romantic comedies, turning on the conflict between love and honour, that soon became an important characteristic of the Spanish Theatre.

Yet there were still no proper theatres. Strolling companies of the 16th century performed in cathedral-squares, market-places, and inn-yards. Cervantes, author of the famous *Don Quixote*, tells us how scanty their equipment was: their whole baggage going into a single sack, their stage consisting of a few planks laid across benches. But by the end of the century there were permanent theatres in Madrid, Seville and Valencia: Many had what we call the 'picture-frame' stage, with a proscenium arch and painted scenery. These theatres of the Spanish 'Golden Age' made use of the kind of stage with which we are all familiar, and this in turn gave the plays, which generally became divided into three acts, a familiar shape.

Life in Spain during this period offered the dramatists plenty of excellent material. It ran to extremes, from the stately magnificence of the Court and the nobles' palaces to the grim poverty of life in many country districts; from aristocratic and high-flown notions of honor to the cynical comic realism of the rogues and vagabonds.

During the first half of this 'Golden Age' the outstanding dramatist was Lope de Vega. It is estimated that he wrote at least 1500 plays, many of them in elaborate verse form. To satisfy the Spanish public's enormous appetite for drama he worked at high pressure, at times completing a play in a single day, with messengers from the stage-manager waiting to carry off the sheets as soon as he had finished them. Yet his best remaining plays have genuine merit.

Towering above the many playwrights who came between was Calderon, one of the world's great dramatic poets. Calderon was a master of stagecraft as well as the poet of sumptuous verse. He would turn with ease from allegory, from the religious parables of the autos which he never ceased to write, to powerful plays in a realistic setting, like his *Mayor of Zalamea*. But his most valuable contributions to world drama are probably his deeply poetic plays, especially *The Wonderful Magician* and *Life is a Dream*. With Calderon this 'Golden Age' of the Spanish Theatre ends in a sunset blaze of glory.

England's Elizabethan Theatre developed rapidly during the triumphant years following the defeat of the Spanish Armada. For some time, troupes of professional players, the retainers of wealthy nobles, had toured the country to increase their masters' prestige. There was also amateur performing of Moralities and knockabout folk-entertainment. The professional actor-managers – including Shakespeare – who eventually built and ran the London playhouses, still looked to the Court and important noblemen for their permits to perform, but they had to attract popular audiences. These wanted clowning and sword-combats, but had a genuine passion for quickness of wit and poetry spoken with fire and feeling.

The Elizabethan stage was admirably designed to please a quickwitted and imaginative audience. It consisted of a forestage, jutting into the audience, on which outdoor scenes were played; a curtained inner stage to suggest interiors; and an upper stage or balcony. Because there was no scenery to be changed, no curtain to be lowered, the dramatist could move freely and swiftly from place to place. Having only words at his command for description of time, place and atmosphere, the dramatist had to use his imagination and compelled his audience to use theirs. All had to be done by the poet and the actors (who, including the boys who played the women's parts, were thoroughly trained and accomplished). As he delivered one of the famous speeches (written as great solos for the voice, like arias in opera) the actor on the forestage had an intimate relation with his audience, perhaps impossible to recapture on our picture-frame stage. We put the actor in another world, at which we stare through the frame of the proscenium arch; Elizabethan Theatre brought the actor into our world, creating dramatic experience of a kind never since achieved.

There is no room here fully to discuss the poetic genius of Shakespeare, the most gifted human being who ever put pen to paper. But, apart from silly theories that will not accept Shakespeare the actor as the author of the plays, there are two mistaken ideas about Shakespeare that must be mentioned.

The first, popular among the neo-classical critic of the 18th century, was that he was a kind of inspired barbarian, hardly knowing what he was doing. The second wrong view of him, which we owe to the romantic critics of the 19th century, suggests that every line he ever wrote is heavy with profound meaning, that he was infallibly wiser than we are, and incapable of careless writing.

Even if Ben Jonson had not told us that Shakespeare wrote his plays quickly, we could have guessed that he did simply because he wrote so much (besides acting and, later, helping to manage a company) in so short a time. Often he was careless and lost interest in what he was doing. Again, he preferred to take his plots from stories of older plays, and sometimes he got into a muddle because he put too much into a character for the part that character had to play in the action. In *The Merchant of Venice* Shylock becomes too human for the villainous part he has to play. Falstaff grew so much bigger and better than he was intended to be that Shakespeare had to 'kill him off' in *Henry V*. It is more than likely that the character of Hamlet has bewildered so many critics just because most of what he does belongs to an older play, whereas the superb things Hamlet says are very much Shakespeare himself.

He wrote always out of prevailing moods; and it *is* easy to discover what these were from the language, the sort of imagery, that he used. The plays show him to us beginning in confident high spirits, then doubting and questioning, then discovering depths of disgust and horror, finally recovering himself: taking it easy in his retirement, telling the romantic fairy stories of *The Winter's Tale* and *The Tempest*.

Having an extraordinary, rich nature, Shakespeare was divided and contradictory about many things. For instance, he believed in law and order and sober conduct and a sense of duty, but he could not help feeling some sympathy with rebellious and raffish characters, whether comic like Falstaff, or tragic like Antony and Cleopatra. But then he would not have been the supreme master of drama he was if he had not had this astonishing breadth of sympathy, creating contradictions and a tug-of-war in his mind.

Other dramatists bring important characters, big scenes to life; but Shakespeare can bring the smallest characters and the tiniest scenes equally to life. And though he often seems careless and casual, just flinging one little scene after another at us, more often than not he is building up his drama, with its own world, its own atmosphere, by one wonderful little stroke after another. It is this combination of unique breadth of sympathy and intense dramatic life that makes Shakespeare the supreme master of the Theatre of any age or any nation.

There was more dramatic talent in the London of Elizabeth and James I than there has ever been since in that city or any other. To name only a few: Marlowe, a tragic poet of strange wild power; Ben Jonson, whose best comedies are superbly written and crammed with rich speech; Dekker, excellent in comedy and in his romantic-pathetic women characters; Middleton and Heywood, with their bustling plays of contemporary life; the tragic and sinister Webster; Massinger, an adroit master of effective acting scenes; and Beaumont and Fletcher, ingenious, versatile and very successful.

But the real Elizabethan Theatre, with its packed pits, its comic breadth, its poetic grandeur, its tremendous vitality, had vanished before Shakespeare died in 1616. The old playhouses, unroofed and giving their performances only during daylight, had made way for covered theatres playing in the evening by the artificial light of candles.

Under James I there was not the same popular enthusiasm for the drama. The Puritans, rapidly increasing in numbers and influence, hated the Theatre which retaliated by burlesquing them and making the most of its threatened freedom. But the theatres closed by the Puritan Parliamentary Ordinance of 1642 had little of the vitality and value of the original Elizabethan Theatre.

As the drama proper declined during the reigns of James I and Charles I, the Masque claimed more and more attention. The Masque originated in renaissance Italy, and during the 16th century found its way first to the French, then to the English Court. It was essentially a court entertainment, designed to be what we should call now an 'after-dinner show' on splendid occasions. It had no real dramatic structure. Poets wrote complimentary verses to be spoken in it, but it mostly consisted of song-and-dance scenes, which, under the two Stuart kings, were often lavishly produced, being magnificently mounted and dressed.

By encouraging scene designers and painters, the use of rich and fantastic costumes, the invention of stage machinery, the Masque undoubtedly made possible the later production of opera and ballet.

But if we regard the Theatre as the home of truly imaginative drama, the creator of real dramatic experience, the Masque did it more harm than good. For what it gave to the eye, what it did to satisfy the idle curiosity and wonder of its spectators, it took away from imagination.

From Venice to Weimar

In the period between 1650–1750 (often called 'neoclassical' as it copied the tastes of classical Rome) France, with its dominating position, and magnificent Court of Versailles, took the lead in the Theatre. But France owed a great deal to Italy. Two types of drama found their way into Italian Theatre: one scholarly, the other popular.

In fifteenth-century Italy, Greek scholars, escaping from the Turks, settled and taught in academies.

Generations ahead of the rest of Europe, Italy revived classical drama – especially Greek New Comedy and Latin imitations of it by Plautus and Terence. Famous Italian authors, notably Ariosto, Machiavelli, Bruno, wrote comedies based on classical models, though inventing characters of their own times. Satirical, topical writers showed what could be done with situations from ordinary life. Meanwhile Italian architects developed stages and auditoriums which led European theatrical design for two centuries.

The popular contribution came from the unique Italian *commedia dell' arte*, possibly the old Mime come to life again. Traces of it remain to this day in the Harlequinade and Punch-

and-Judy. Its masked characters, played by women as well as men, were mostly stock comic figures: the foolish old man, swaggering soldier, interfering servants. *Commedia* dialogue was improvised by the quick-witted players. But scenes followed a definite plot.

This popular comic drama was imported into France, where an Italian company played for over a century. Thus on both scholarly and popular levels first credit must go to Italy for founding a neoclassical Theatre in Europe.

The neoclassical French Theatre succeeded more in comedy than tragedy in an age which preferred to ignore those dark corners of the mind from which romantic literature emerges. It did not want a writer to record ideas private and peculiar to himself; it wanted him to express something everyone agreed about. All this helped satirical comedy, mocking absurd fashions and current affectations. The Theatre, entertaining a comparatively small Court society with frequent new satirical productions, is at such a time almost like a comic periodical.

This Theatre gave us Molière, the world's greatest writer of classical artificial comedy. After touring the provinces for 12 years with his own company, Molière returned to Paris and was fortunate in obtaining the patronage of Louis XIV.

At this time a satirical dramatist in France was in a difficult position. If he offended the Court or the Church, the Theatre was closed to him and he might find himself under arrest. The Theatre owes something to Louis XIV for his patronage and protection of Molière; but if Molière had written in a freer society, his drama might have been even richer.

It was his duty to provide not only straight comedies but mixed pieces with songs and ballet. But his Theatre was not elaborate and spectacular; he worked mostly on a small and fairly simple scale, rarely with large casts, using the street and interior scenes common in this kind of comedy.

Molière has two outstanding qualities as a dramatist. The first is his inventive ingenuity, enabling him to make an effective comedy out of almost any fad or fashion. He was a wonderful contriver for the stage, giving every stroke its effect, every speech its sharp point. He knew his business as few dramatists have known theirs.

But it is his outstanding human quality that lifts him high above the other writers of artificial comedy. This quality comes from a kind of delicate balance in him of reason and feeling. Molière could create characters that may be taking part in a satire but for all that are not merely caricatures but have life and depth. Some of his more ambitious plays, such as *Le Misanthrope*, *Tartuffe* and *Don Juan*, are far from being artificial comedies of the usual kind, having much of the penetration and insight into life of the best serious drama. And even his lighter satirical pieces – sheer absurdities, burlesquing what seemed to him pretentious and inflated in the Parisian society he knew – never outrage as the plays of lesser comic playwrights do, the dignity and decency of life.

Desperately overworked and never in good health, unfortunate in his domestic life, responsible and anxious, Molière was far from being a happy man; but no man in his time, and very few since, brought as much wit and sparkling inventiveness into the Theatre and made so many others happy.

French neoclassical tragedy in the 17th century was a drama governed by strict rules. The most important of these were the famous Unities, supposedly derived from Aristotle's Poetics but actually more severe than anything he had laid down.

It was decided that a true tragedy, obeying the Unities, would develop a single story (with no subplots), would use only one scene, and assume no greater passage of time than that taken by the play's performance. A further rule, less strictly observed, was that violent action should not be shown to the audience, but merely described to it.

Excellent drama, highly concentrated and tense, can be created within these rules. But the French classical theorists went wrong in imposing them on every tragic dramatist. They took much of the breadth and force and poetic grandeur out of tragedy – and indeed a great deal of its reality.

The single scene became a vague antechamber, apparently belonging to nobody, too public for all the confidences exchanged in it. Often the time restriction meant so many crises happened close together that what ought to have been tragic became ludicrous. So much had to be described instead of seen that all the chief characters had to be provided with confidants and messengers – so many dummies in place of real characters. As tragedy must be kept high and mighty and not show or mention any homely familiar thing, significant details were missing from it, giving it an abstract, unreal air.

An additional problem was posed by the fashionable gentlemen, ever ready to titter or sneer at a dramatist who showed ignorance of the correct neoclassic rules, who occupied seats actually on the stage. They must have embarrassed the tragic poet and his actors.

But Pierre Corneille's most famous play, *Le Cid*, did not entirely conform to the rules, and indeed Corneille, a romantic at heart, was never at ease with them. He had a good sense of the Theatre, though unless thoroughly roused by a big scene, a great moment, he could be prosy and rather tedious. But when challenged by that scene, that moment, his lines could be wonderfully sonorous and fiery.

Racine, much younger, was perfectly at home with the rules and even refined them, perfecting a poetic classical style, using plain language, yet with haunting cadences and undertones. He employed few characters, cut down the action to what was strictly necessary, but was searching and subtle in creating his chief characters, especially the women. Tragic actresses still covet the role of Racine's *Phèdre*.

His themes and personages are historical, but Racine makes little attempt to create the atmosphere of a period in history, to show us another age coming alive. It is hard to feel that these tragic characters are the Roman emperors and queens of Palestine we are told they are, and not eloquent ladies and gentlemen from the Court of Louis XIV.

The English Theatre began again soon after the Restoration of the Monarchy in 1660 when *Charles II* granted patents – permits to produce plays – to only two companies of players. When, much later, other theatres opened, their managers included song-and-dance scenes in their productions which were therefore not 'straight plays' needing a permit.

The two companies introduced actresses to play the female parts, and performed chiefly for the Court – the small, fashionable world. The Theatre was not rooted in national life as it had been under Elizabeth, and the wonderfully flexible Elizabethan stage had been replaced by the picture-frame stage on the Continental model.

The Restoration Theatre had its tragic dramatists, but the taste of the time made comedy far more important. There have been many critical disputes about these Restoration comedies. Some people condemn them for their monotony and indecency. Others consider them too artificial to be taken seriously as pictures of life and enjoy them simply as exhibitions of wit and comic character.

Wycherley, the coarsest, and perhaps the least witty of the early Restoration dramatists, is on the stage the most effective, for he had great dramatic vitality, and a fine eye for a droll character and an uproarious scene. But for style and wit, especially in his final comedy, *The Way of the World*, Congreve is the master of them all. In his best scenes, his brilliant style has never been surpassed in English comedy. The Theatre lost most by the early death of George Farquhar, whose *The Recruiting Officer* and frequently revived *The Beaux Stratagem* successfully broke away from the narrow artificial comedy of manners, took the scene from London into the country, and brought a breezy freshness into a comedy that was turning stale.

The English Theatre had to wait nearly 70 years for comedy as good as Farquhar's. Then came two Irishmen: Goldsmith and Sheridan. Goldsmith's first comedy, *The Good-Natured Man*, was a failure, but his second, *She Stoops to Conquer*, has triumphantly held the stage since its first appearance. Its central plot, a young man mistaking a private house for an inn, was not original and is wildly unconvincing; but the play is written with such gusto that it still captivates audiences.

Sheridan, who in spite of being in politics contrived to manage Drury Lane for many years, wrote only two outstanding comedies, both while he was young: *The Rivals* and *The School for Scandal*.

The Rivals has the fresher wit, the more unforced youthful gaiety, but *The School for Scandal* has been revived more frequently than any comedy written by any playwright since Shakespeare.

The chief developments in European Theatre during the first three-quarters of the 18th century are a change in audiences and their taste, and revolt against dominating French influence, all-powerful during the early years of the century.

In Scandinavia, when by 1737 Stockholm had its Royal Theatre, French influence was still paramount; but Holberg, who directed the Danish Theatre, created a lively Danish-Norwegian style.

In Russia, French, German and Italian companies paid long visits and it was not until the last quarter of the century that a native Russian drama grew up. In Germany, visiting French companies played their classics at the larger courts, while

German companies, playing popular stuff with plenty of clowning, amused the townsfolk. English companies, which had had a great reputation during the Elizabethan age, no longer toured Europe; however, in 1752 the first professional London company crossed the sea to Williamsburg, Virginia, which, like New York, Philadelphia and Charleston, already had a playhouse of a sort.

Meanwhile, in London itself, the regular audiences were no longer merely composed of the upper class. The solid middle class, making up family parties, now patronised the playhouses; and these people did not want witty indecencies but plays with plenty of melodramatic action and sentiment. They were chiefly catered for by George Lillo, his greatest hit being *The London Merchant or The History of George Barnwell* – an unfortunate youth who, falling in love with a bad woman, murdered his rich old uncle.

In Paris, the most famous author of the age, Voltaire, was creating a new fashion by writing 'tragedies', very different from Racine's, which demanded spectacular effects in exotic settings. It was his *Semiramis* that finally cleared once privileged spectators off the stage in France.

The new movement, then, responding to the change of audiences and taste, went in two directions. In one, it replaced artificial comedies with sentimental domestic plays appealing to middle-class families. In the other, it moved towards larger theatres with deeper, wider stages where, instead of formal tragedies, these new audiences were offered plays with plenty of action, numerous scenes, crowds of Incas, Aztecs, Chinese, Turks, and grand, spectacular effects including battle-scenes, temples on fire, waterfalls and rivers in glittering motion.

At the same time there were literary influences at work, destined to play an important part in the whole European Theatre. The first, and less important, was the publication of old ballads and folk-songs like Bishop Percy's *Reliques of*

Ancient English Poetry. Particularly in central and northern Europe these encouraged a romantic taste for the past and for folk-poetry; a taste that was not destined to remain long outside the Theatre.

The second influence, of immense importance, was the discovery of Shakespeare by foreign scholars; then, through their translations, by foreign dramatists, critics, actors and managers who found themselves staring into a whole new magic world of drama – tragic, comic, historical, fantastic. Young dramatists in one country after another (with Germany in the lead) became fascinated by this newly revealed magic and found a new way, far removed from classical formality, of writing for the Theatre.

The English, Spanish and French Theatres reached their peaks during the century that began about 1590. At no time did the German Theatre reach such eminence, but towards the end of the 18th century it took the European lead.

The father of this Theatre was Lessing, himself both critic and dramatist. With his more important plays like *Minna von Barnhelm*, which dealt with contemporary German life, *Emilia Galotti*, a tragedy of middle-class life, and *Nathan the Wise*, a parable play about religious tolerance, Lessing awakened Germany to the possibilities of its Theatre.

Lessing's challenge was accepted by two poets of genius: Goethe and Schiller. After a wild start during what became called the *Sturm und Drang* – Storm and Stress – period (after a play of that name), they settled near each other and separately raised German poetic drama to a lofty height.

Goethe, the foremost German writer, was appointed Minister of State by the Duke of Weimar and Director of the Duke's private theatre. This small dukedom was not wealthy. Goethe had to make the most of a badly-equipped playhouse, old scenery and costumes, and an inadequate company of undistinguished, overworked, underpaid players. Moreover, although Goethe wrote plays of wonderful poetic quality and had a fine taste in drama, he was not at heart a man of the Theatre. *Iphigenia* and *Torquato Tasso* are too slow moving, *Egmont* lacks true dramatic development, and *Faust*, though a literary masterpiece, makes too many demands upon the Theatre's resources. However, Goethe made little Weimar the capital of European Theatre.

Schiller, like Racine in France, has always had a greater reputation at home than abroad. For eloquent and firmly constructed historical tragedy, he was certainly unmatched in his Romantic age. His most ambitious work, a trilogy of plays based on the life of Count Wallenstein, has never been widely played outside Germany, but his *Don Carlos*, *Maria Stuart*, *William Tell*, have taken possession of many stages in many countries. His dramatic virtues stem from his generous idealism, eloquence and feeling for theatrical effect. He lacks what Shakespeare possesses in abundance: a sense of poetic historical atmosphere and sharply individual characterisation.

The efforts of Goethe and Schiller at Weimar soon raised the level of the whole German Theatre which then produced some fine dramatists. Ever since Goethe was at Weimar the Theatre has been firmly rooted in German national and civic life. No other country can show us so many well-organised and dignified municipal playhouses – excellent models for what ought to be done, but has not yet been seriously attempted, in America and Britain.

Eastern Stages

Except in the Far East, the Asian peoples have not had a flourishing, highly-developed Theatre. This may seem surprising since they have devoted themselves to poetry, story-telling, singing, dancing and the decorative arts. There are two possible explanations. One is that Asia's monastic religions have attracted the types of thinkers who have created great drama elsewhere, leaving them no opportunity to consider the matter at all. The second, certainly true of India, is that the progress of drama was checked by Mohammedan invasions.

Hindu drama belongs to Sanskrit literature and it was an English translation of one of its classics (*Sakuntala*, by its best dramatist, Kalidasa) appearing in the late 18th century, that turned the attention of Europeans to Sanskrit literature. The origins of Hindu drama are not known. Possibly Greek invaders under Alexander the Great suggested the idea of drama; but it arrived at its best period, with Kalidasa, in about the fifth century AD.

Actors belonged to a special caste of no great dignity, and moved around with a leader; a kind of actor-manager who also introduced the play to the audience. There were no proper theatres and most performances took place, under the patronage of the local ruler, in a palace or temple. There was no scenery, just a curtain covering the back of the stage. Costumes and make-up were formal and traditional, indicating the caste, nationality, type of character. A few stage properties, some 'noises off' and similar simple effects were used.

The plays were mostly based on stories from familiar myths and legends. They contained quite a wide variety of characters and some charming touches of drama, but would seem to Western playgoers too literary; needing more intrigue, action and dramatic interest. But two of these old Hindu plays, *Sakuntala*, already mentioned, and *The Toy Cart*, have been produced with some success in Western playhouses. After a very long interval of neglect, this classical Sanskrit drama was translated into Bengali and revived. Now, both Indian and Western plays are produced in the Indian Theatre.

Will the traditional Chinese Theatre, which has reached us almost unchanged after many centuries, survive the Communist regime, hurrying to modernise and Westernise everything? We can only hope so, for this ancient Chinese art makes a highly original contribution to world Theatre.

Watching a traditional Chinese production we might at first be more sharply aware of its originality than capable of enjoying it. The orchestra, harsh and explosive to our ears, plays a great part in this Theatre, heightening the climaxes and setting the tempo for entrances and exits.

The elaborate costumes, and equally elaborate and far more startling make-up, are formal and traditional and indicate exactly who a character is. For instance, a famous brigand chief has a striking dark blue face, scarlet eyebrows and beard, and an extra pair of eyes painted below his own.

There is no scenery. The stage, projecting squarely into the auditorium, is curtained at back and sides – one side for entrances, the other for exits. Stage properties are few and simple but symbolic and highly conventional. A table and chair can represent anything from actual furniture to a fortress. Black flags indicate a high wind, flags with waves on them suggest water; an actor carrying an oar is imagined to be in a boat, one who brandishes a horse-whip is supposed to be riding a horse. To suggest an army entering a city, a few actors carrying large banners (symbolising military grandeur) march by a painted arch held up by property men, who, dressed in black and presumed to be invisible, are frequently busy on the stage.

When the audience is to imagine a change of scene, the actors walk round in a circle. This may happen many times because the plays are immensely long and very episodic, capable of suggesting whole epics of adventure. It is here, in the length and looseness of structure, that the chief weakness of this Theatre lies. The dramatist's art hardly reaches its height in such immense, wandering melodramas, complete with morals and happy endings.

But in Chinese drama the actor's art is richly and wonderfully represented. Most of us who have seen Chinese actors have been entranced simply by their miming – for example, pretending to fight with swords in a dark room or to row a boat – and this is only part of their training which includes manipulation of the voice for tragic or comic purposes, and highly stylised gestures in which the wave of a finger may carry a weight of meaning. Actors playing female roles must be particularly skilled.

With this extremely conventional and simplified method of staging a play, there is little or nothing to distract attention from the actors. They are not only acting the scenes but creating the world in which the scenes are taking place.

There is much to be said for a Theatre of this kind, with staging so economical, flexible, imaginative. [...] The Chinese took this convention as far as it will go. Is it possible we have something to learn from them?

Surprising as it may seem to those who do not know them, the Japanese are very theatrical. They are an excitable people pretending to be very calm; bringing to their whole national life a certain histrionic element. There is more than a hint of the Theatre in their conventional costumes, carefully arranged backgrounds and settings, and stylised ceremonies: and they are extremely fond of the Theatre itself, including modern plays imported from the West.

The national Theatre in Japan consists of three forms of drama: the No, the oldest, most distinguished and elaborate form; the Kabuki, or popular Theatre; and the marionettes. The No plays, partly religious in origin, traditional and highly conventional in style, essentially aristocratic, would seem to Western audiences like some small-scale ceremonial kind of opera. The orchestra and singers, seated on the not-very-large square stage, play a great part in these performances. One device of these plays, disconcerting to a Western spectator, is to split the time-effect; keeping the action (for instance the approach of a new character) at the slowest of slow-motion speeds, while the orchestra and singers suggest rapidity and urgency. The women's parts are played by specially trained male performers. It is a drama for connoisseurs, simple enough in the stories it tells, but very elaborate and stylised in its ritual of performance.

The Kabuki Theatre, designed to entertain the mass of people who found the atmosphere of the No plays too rarefied, is very different. Its stage is not very high or deep, but is extraordinarily wide. On a 'runway' extending from it to the back of the auditorium, characters can make extremely effective entrances and exits. Scenes are solid and realistic, and many of the stage effects – for instance, a village on fire – would be the envy of Western stage managers. The acting, both in the heightened tragic manner and the realistic comic style, is very good indeed. The players, again with no women among them, do not wear masks, as the chief actors in the No plays do, but are heavily made-up. Incidental music is used rather as the Theatre orchestra used to be in 19th-century Western melo-dramas. Kabuki performances last much longer than ours and frequently scenes from several plays are given. Though Western drama is increasingly popular, new Kabuki plays, based on the old traditional stories, are still being written.

The third Japanese form, the marionettes, must not be confused with the kind of puppet-show familiar to us. The dolls are almost lifesize figures, very elaborately articulated; and each important one requires three trained men to manipulate it. Though these are visible, it is not difficult even for a Western newcomer to ignore their existence and to concentrate on the astonishingly graceful and significant movements and gestures of these marionette characters. The stage, much smaller than the Kabuki stage, is quite elaborately set, and its scenery is designed to enable the manipulators and their marionettes to move along different levels. The action of the pieces they perform is described by five singers accompanied by stringed instruments. But there is far less popular interest in this highly artificial type of Theatre and the very rapid development of film production in Japan is itself a threat to all three forms of the traditional Japanese Theatre.

Romance and Realism

The first half of the 19th century was on the whole a curiously uneventful period in the history of the European Theatre. It is typical of the earlier part of this age that the new plays most widely and successfully produced were those of a German, Kotzebue, whose work is now forgotten. They were in fact large spectacular melodramas adroitly contrived to please the taste of the popular audiences, and to show off the many resources of the big theatres these audiences filled. These pieces, which usually had an exotic setting, had neither literary nor true dramatic merit but were what is commonly known as 'good Theatre'.

It was not that real poets and men of talent had no interest in the Theatre. Several of the English Romantic poets for example wrote plays, of which the best is probably Shelley's *Cenci*; but somehow they failed to achieve an essential theatrical quality; failed just as mysteriously as the Elizabethan and Jacobean poet-playwrights had succeeded.

Great actors like Edmund Kean in London, Talma in Paris, appeared in revivals of the classics and helped raise the art of acting to a new high level. But drama itself made no progress, in spite of what Goethe and Schiller had accomplished.

Nothing momentous happened in the Theatre until a famous night in 1830 when Victor Hugo's *Hernani* was first produced and caused a riot. Hugo had deliberately broken all the rules of classic restraint and, knowing there would be trouble, took care to bring into the theatre four hundred enthusiastic young men, art students and the like, who supported the new Romantic attitude.

Hugo was a greater poet than playwright, but his act of rebellion brought new life to the French Theatre. So did the exciting historical melodramas of Dumas; though soon to be excelled by those of his son, Dumas *fils*, the author of the famous 'tearjerker' *The Lady of the Camellias*. Less successful at first than any of these, but really a more interesting dramatist, was the poet Alfred de Musset, whose delicate, half-romantic, half-mocking pieces came to be played and enjoyed more and more during the latter half of the century, when the Theatre everywhere gained vitality.

Seated in a box on that riotous first night of Hugo's *Hernani*, a prominent member of the group opposing the poet, was Eugène Scribe. He became the most popular playwright of the period 1830–60, and, with a number of collaborators, is said to have written 400 plays. Scribe was the originator of what was known as the 'well-made' play, and he and his successor, Victorien Sardou, dominated the commercial Theatre in France and elsewhere during the 19th century. It was a Theatre that set out to entertain the comfortable bourgeois classes, on the increase in all the capitals. These audiences were not necessarily foolish, but lacked imagination and never expected the Theatre to tell them anything worth knowing about life.

The trouble with these Scribe-Sardou plays is that they are so much adroit construction and contrivance and little else. They do not spring out of living characters and their circum-stances. They are merely clever concoctions in which effective scenes, startling situations, are thought of first and fitted out with dummy characters.

But right to the end of the 19th century, this type of play, usually staged and acted with considerable skill, took possession of the smaller and more expensive playhouses everywhere; leaving the spectacular melodramas, which for all their crudities had often more dramatic vitality in them, to the larger theatres with plenty of cheap seats in the pit and gallery.

It was these smaller playhouses, designed to attract audiences of the middle and upper classes, that about the middle of the century made changes which helped to create the playhouse as we know it today. In the old theatres were no 'orchestra stalls' or *fauteuils*, now the most expensive seats in the house. The pit, farther below stage level than the stalls are today, occupied the whole floor of the theatre; and the best seats were in the first circle, not then much above stage level. But the new, smaller, more fashionable playhouses pushed the pit to the back, often reducing it to a few rows, and filled the area between it and the stage with comfortable, numbered stalls that could be booked by Theatre-goers in advance.

The large old popular theatres had offered a long, mixed entertainment, often with a full-length play, a few songs, and a short farce as a final item. The new playhouses opened later in the evening, and though a short piece called a 'curtain raiser' might precede the play, the interlude of singing and the final farce were dropped. Because their chief patrons now arrived in evening-dress, these new and more expensive theatres were made cleaner, more comfortable and better ventilated than the big popular theatres had ever been.

As industrial wealth increased throughout the century, so these more luxurious commercial playhouses multiplied on both sides of the Atlantic. But with these theatres disappeared that heightened feeling of being one in an audience; a communal, classless feeling which the big old theatres had known. It needed more than Theatre-going as a social habit to restore vitality to the drama.

Some important developments in the Western Theatre can be illustrated by what happened in London in the 1860s. Tom Robertson, a dramatist who had been an actor, joined forces with Squire Bancroft, an accomplished actor, and his wife, Marie Wilton, an extremely popular actress.

Robertson supplied these two, who were also theatre managers, with a series of plays (*Society*, *Ours*, *Caste*, *Play*, *School*) that were called 'cup-and-saucer' drama because they avoided wildly dramatic scenes, huge flowery speeches, fantastically unreal characters in impossible situations; and successfully attempted a far more realistic type of domestic, sentimental, humorous drama. This was directed with great care by Robertson himself.

Actors, receiving much larger salaries than had been customary, were carefully selected to play particular parts, and rehearsed for some weeks. All this was new. Before, actors had formed part of a stock company, playing many different parts. Rehearsals were few and casual; only the major movements and groupings were worked out, and an experienced actor was assumed to know what to do with himself on the stage.

Robertson insisted on the setting of his plays being realistic: a room had to be exactly the kind of room he described in his text. It could no longer be a large, vague, bare apartment, unconvincingly put together out of side-pieces or 'wings' and a backcloth. It had to look like somebody's room, not nobody's; it had to have walls; it had to be properly decorated and furnished; it had to have doors and windows that opened. This meant the use for all interiors of 'box sets' made up of canvas 'flats' cleated together to form the three walls, of a ceiling and of practicable doors and windows.

The old painted-cloth-and-wings room may not have looked attractive or convincing (do we go to the Theatre to see rooms anyway?) but it never had a piece of furniture that was not essential for the action, it cost very little, would do for almost any play, and could be changed in half a minute. Its painted cloths were 'flown': hoisted into the 'flies' where men, hidden by the proscenium arch, raised and lowered the scenery high above the stage.

The old painted-cloth scenery made repertory easy and inexpensive. It cost little to change plays every night for a week. But the introduction of these box sets, heavily furnished and 'dressed' (as stage managers say) with pictures, ornaments, clocks, et cetera, made repertory difficult and costly. Men like Robertson and Bancroft were preparing for a long run of one play, not for the continuing production of a number of plays. This new realism then, so far as the commercial Theatre (a Theatre not receiving any state or municipal subsidies to help support it) was concerned, almost brought repertory to an end.

As both costs of production and salaries went up, and only a long run brought any profit, managers soon showed less and less desire to be adventurous and experimental in their choice of plays. During the second half of the century the most vital drama was no longer making its first appearance in the wealthiest cities – in London, New York or Paris, where more and more commercial theatres came into existence, producing 'tell-tried plays adapted from the French' of Scribe and Sardou.

Yet, ironically enough, this new drama had not turned away from realism or naturalism in the Theatre, but simply raised it to a higher power.

This new drama came, most unexpectedly, from Norway. Henrik Ibsen (1828–1906), as a young Norwegian beginning to write plays, worked in the Theatre at Bergen and Oslo, received a fellowship, then a state pension but lived out of Norway in Italy and Germany, for most of his life. He was always at heart a poet; and two of his most important earlier dramas, *Brand* and *Peer Gynt*, do not belong to the Theatre of prose realism. But most of his work does, and his tremendous influence on world, as well as Norwegian, Theatre, has been as a dramatist of prose realism.

Ibsen's contribution to the Theatre was two-fold.

He brought to it a deeply searching and serious mind. The issues in an Ibsen play are in fact the most serious issues known to the modern mind. Although he had a natural inclination towards a poetic and symbolic treatment, he realised that the Theatre of his time was committing itself more and more to realism or naturalism, and in his own determined, grimly patient fashion – for he was a grim, determined man – he hammered out a realistic prose technique that beat the Theatre at its own game.

This brings us to his second contribution. He took the 'well-made' play, charged it with high seriousness instead of triviality, and made it technically even better. He did it by a severe concentration of the action. Instead of showing his characters in a series of scenes leading to a crisis as other dramatists had done, he began his most characteristic plays just before the crisis arrived, made his audience acquainted with what had gone before by talk dramatic in itself – between his characters, and then devoted the main part of his play to a resolving of the crisis.

This method gave an Ibsen drama a richness and dramatic urgency immensely rewarding to audiences prepared to use their intelligence and release their emotions, distasteful to this day to people who merely want to giggle or doze in the playhouse.

Though Ibsen's originality and greatness cannot be questioned, he has limitations. His characters share Ibsen's humourless nature; and his creation of character, though searching and profound, is rather narrowly based for the greatest dramatist of his age.

Oddly enough, the only possible challenge to his pre-eminence also comes from Scandinavia, in the person of August Strindberg (1849–1912), a Swede. Strindberg may have learnt some of his fine technique from Ibsen, but their plays are very different. A far more unbalanced man, close to insanity at times, Strindberg is more unequal than Ibsen, though also even more versatile. In certain of his plays, like *The Father*, within a convincingly realistic framework he can produce drama of almost appalling intensity; in some plays his psychological subtlety is even superior to Ibsen's.

Both dramatists are held to have brought into existence the 'problem' play. But a great dramatist does not solve 'whodunnit' problems. He may create for us a certain kind of dramatic experience involving religious, philosophical, social or political issues which are an important part of our lives; but he leaves us to settle these problems ourselves.

Realism for realism's sake probably reached its peak with the New York manager, David Belasco, who thought nothing of putting an exact replica of a restaurant on the stage. But this was showmanship.

The finest examples of complete naturalism – interpreting the play's texts – could be found in Moscow in the early years of this century. They were the productions of the Moscow Art Theatre, founded in 1898 by Stanislavski and Nemirovich-Danchenko, who were both dissatisfied by the artificial style of acting then existing in Russia.

Older realistic playwrights like Ostrovski needed a less mannered style of acting; and promising new writers like Chekhov could not be properly produced at all in the existing manner. Two visits by the Meiningen Company from Germany, famous for its settings, crowd-acting and the accuracy and finish of its productions, had convinced many Russians that new theatrical companies, methods of training actors and staging plays were needed. The Moscow Art Theatre was easily the greatest of these new companies, and it still is.

It will always be associated with the name of Chekhov, one of the most original and subtle of all dramatists. He disregarded every rule of playwriting. He is not telling anybody's story. He is not showing a conflict between determined characters. Instead of having more will-power than most of us, his characters have less.

There is no conflict, no crisis, no climax. He says in effect, 'This is what life was like to this group of people.' In place of the familiar dramatic excitement he gives us a wonderful depth of character and scene: humorous, pathetic, tender. When his people are eloquent, they are merely showing off and being silly. When they truly reveal themselves, they do it in a few casual, broken phrases.

It is the only drama that seems to have more inconsequence than real life. But it is composed with consummate art. Its naturalism is a poetic naturalism. This is the key to the Moscow Art Theatre productions of Chekhov; built up slowly, with great elaboration.

All manner of effects are introduced – a bird singing, a train passing, distant music, and so forth – but not for reality's sake. Like the beautiful lighting of these plays, they create atmosphere, heighten the emotion of a scene, 'orchestrate' the author's text.

In these Moscow Art Theatre productions of Chekhov with their special training of actors, endless rehearsals, immense care for every detail of the sets, costume, make-up, intricate blending of speech and movement, lighting effects, the Theatre reached the summit of naturalism. This was not showmanship but an attempt to suggest inside the Theatre the wealth of sight and sound, the sudden humor, the hidden heartbreak, the largely unspoken poetry of this life of ours.

Ideas and Experiments

So far during this century the Theatre has shown us a great deal of experiment and an increasing variety of styles – in writing, stage design, acting and production – rather than a continued development of one style, as in earlier centuries.

Non-commercial and experimental theatrical companies have been dominated far more by directors and dramatists than by star actors managing their own companies. For instance, the famous Abbey Theatre in Dublin was run first by W B Yeats, a great poet, and Lady Gregory, a playwright, and afterwards by Lennox Robinson, another playwright. This was essentially a national theatre, designed to produce Irish drama; and it gave us such fine dramatists as Synge and Sean O'Casey. In America, the Provincetown Players were associated with Eugene O'Neill, then a young dramatist.

In Germany and Russia during the 1920s the Theatre was wildly experimental, making a clean break both in writing and production with realism. In Berlin there was much enthusiasm for a style called Expressionism, in which the characters were very broad types (called simply 'The Man' or 'The Girl') and the action was symbolic, dream-like and not realistic. In Paris new groups abandoned the style of the Boulevard playhouses for the sensitive realism of plays by Vildrac and Jean-Jacques Bernard, or the poetic drama of Andre Obey.

The greatest British dramatist, Bernard Shaw, experimented only in the subject-matter of his plays; and although some producing groups tried experiments for special performances, there was less breaking away from realism in London than in most other capitals.

Though the passion for experiment-at-all-costs of Berlin and Moscow in the 1920s has not been duplicated elsewhere, during the last twenty years there has been a gradual broadening, with T S Eliot and Christopher Fry succeeding with poetic drama, and with Arthur Miller and Tennessee Williams in New York, Giraudoux, Sartre, and Anouilh in Paris – all trying new forms of prose drama; giving apparent realism a poetic intensity. But no unique style has been developed that completely represents and essentially belongs to our age.

Early in this century revolt against realistic painted sets was led by two designers of great talent: Gordon Craig, an Englishman and Adolphe Appia, a Swiss. Both abolished fussy realistic detail, made their set symbolic in form and colouration and tried to give their actors different levels on which to perform. Other directors and designers began to substitute solid three-dimensional shapes, often quite unrealistic, for painted cloths.

In the wildly experimental Theatre of Soviet Russia during the 1920s, a director called Meierhold devised a fantastic style known as 'Constructivism'. All suggestion of realism was replaced by ladders, bridges, bits of machinery, as if the stage designer had nothing to work with but a giant meccano set.

Europe's smaller experimental theatres made more and more use of the Elizabethan forestage or 'apron'. Especially in Shakespearean productions playhouses with conventional stages used permanent sets that could suggest indoor and outdoor scenes by small changes like drawing a curtain.

Another method was to have nothing on the stage but a semicircular stretched cloth or a plaster cyclorama at the back. On this a camera would project scenes painted on slides. But such scenes tend to look thin and unconvincing.

In modern plays demanding rapid changes of scene, directors often used a 'multiple set' with several small interior or even exterior scenes; and picked out with spot-lights the part of the set in use, keeping the rest as dark as possible.

Today most large new theatres have either revolving stages, which simply swing into view the scene to be used, or machinery to raise and lower a large central section of the stage.

We do not go to the playhouse to stare at stage sets but to watch actors and listen to words; so there is something to be said for arena playhouses, or theatres-in-the-round, where the picture-frame notion of the stage is replaced by a stage like the ring of a circus, with no scenery at all. Its advantages lie in its inexpensive working, its intimate relation between actor and audience, and its increased demand upon the imagination of the spectators.

There are now stages which can become picture-frame stages, part picture-frame with forestage or steps going down to the audience, or not picture-frame at all but close replicas of the Elizabethan stage – three theatres for the price of one.

[...]

During the last 30 years the Theatre has had to meet three challenges – from radio, cinema, and television. All three produce drama of a sort; all possess important advantages.

As a rule it does not cost as much to see a film as it does to see a play; and films can be seen in a great many places that have never known a theatre. Radio and television can be enjoyed at home, with a minimum of effort, turning the living-room into a playhouse. And all three, because they are produced for a mass audience, can offer casts of players that only the best theatres could afford.

Outside America it is doubtful if the Theatre yet has had to meet all the competition that television drama can offer it, for this new form of drama is only in an early fumbling stage of its career. But already many people tell us that with their television sets at home and an occasional visit to the movies, they no longer need the Theatre and do not care whether it lives or dies.

Such people do not understand that the Theatre is the parent of these new dramatic forms. Without a living Theatre where writers, directors, designers and actors could learn their jobs, movies and television plays would be very crude indeed. Unfortunately the wealthy organisations responsible for films, radio and television, have helped themselves liberally to the talent the Theatre has trained but have given it little in return. In fact their competition has made the position of the Theatre which has no state support far more precarious than it used to be, and has made commercial theatre managers more reluctant than ever to experiment.

However, as these mass-media do some things better than the Theatre, they might be said to be narrowing but purifying its outlook. An obvious example is the disappearance from the stage of the old spectacular melodrama with its sinking ships, houses on fire, horses racing – simply because this can all be done much better by the film studios.

But there are equally important and more subtle results of this competition. For instance, because the best film dialogue tends to be laconic and rather dry, a certain richness of speech has returned to the Theatre, thus making the most of what it does best.

Again, though television drama is still in its infancy, it is clear that what succeeds most in this medium is drama consisting of intimate scenes between two or three characters; carefully rather than richly written and acted. It is happier with rather small but intensely sincere parts and performances than with extremes of comedy and tragedy acted by impressive personalities.

The Theatre can afford certain grandiose qualities that seem embarrassing in the cold searching light of television. We may expect, then, that quiet, intimate naturalism in writing and acting will appear more and more in television drama, and less and less in the Theatre which will begin to recover its old swagger and style and larger-than-life character.

In a very good restaurant we have a dinner that is specially cooked for us; in a canteen we are merely served with standard portions of a standard meal. And this is the difference between the living Theatre and the mass entertainment of films, radio and television. In the Theatre the play is specially cooked for us. Those who have worked in the Theatre know that a production never takes its final shape until it has an audience.

With films, radio, television, the vast audience can only receive what it is being offered. But in the Theatre the audience might be said to be creatively receptive; its very presence, an intensely living presence, heightens the drama.

The actors are not playing to microphones and cameras but to warmly responsive fellow-creatures.

And they are never giving exactly the same performance. If the audience tends to be heavy, unresponsive – on a wet Monday, perhaps – the company slightly sharpens and heightens its performance to bring the audience to life; and vice versa if the audience is too enthusiastic.

It is the presence of an audience that teaches an actor the essential art of 'timing'. If in comedy the speeches are badly timed; if the actors try to get too many laughs instead of checking little laughs, in order to build up to a huge roar, the keen edge of the audience's attention will be obviously blunted, and the production will not succeed. An actor with talent and long experience always has a wonderful sense of what can be done with an audience; half commanding and half cajoling it to enjoy every moment of his performance.

Film and television acting is much smaller and quieter than that of the Theatre. Nevertheless, with a very few exceptions, the best performers on film and television are actors and actresses from the Theatre, which has taught them their art.

It is the ancient but ever-youthful parent of all entertainment in dramatic form. Much of its work, especially under commercial conditions, may often be trivial and tawdry; but this means that the Theatre should be rescued from such conditions. For in itself, as it has existed on and off for two and a half thousand years, the Theatre is anything but trivial and tawdry. It is the magical place where man meets his image. It is the enduring home of 'dramatic experience', which is surely one of the most searching, rewarding, enchanting of our many different kinds of experience.

1959 (first published in an illustrated edition)

INSPIRATION

IN DESCRIBING how he came to write Time and the Conways, *my father wrote:*

I was lunching with my sister, who was staying with us in Highgate during Whitsuntide, and we were idly discussing old acquaintances and especially a family I had known before the War. Suddenly I saw that there was a play in the relation between a fairly typical middle-class family and the theory of Time, the theory chiefly associated with J W Dunne, over which I had been brooding for the past two years. The idea was not the usual possible good idea one jots down in a notebook and then leaves for a year or two. It excited me at once, and I had to begin sketching out the general action of the play. Within a day or two, having come down here to the Isle of Wight, I had made out a list of the characters and told myself what sort of people they were. The first and third acts were set in 1919, and I needed some 'period' details for these scenes; but I could not wait until we returned to London, where I could do my little bit of research, so I left the two 1919 acts and plunged boldly into the contemporary one, Act Two. With almost no preparation, without any of the usual brooding and note-making, I wrote this Act Two of *Time and the Conways* at full speed. It seemed to cost me no more thought and trouble than if I were dashing off a letter to an old friend. Page after page, scene after scene, went off effortlessly, with hardly a correction on my typescript. I did not stay up late at night, drink strong coffee, put wet towels on my head; I kept bank clerk's hours and almost behaved like one; and yet within two days I had finished this long and complicated act; and what I wrote then, with only two or three tiny alterations, was rehearsed, played, and afterwards printed.

Now this has been said to be one of the most brilliant second acts of our time. Even people who did not care for the play as a whole were enthusiastic about this act. When I came to watch it being rehearsed, I saw that I had solved some very difficult technical problems, and, indeed, that writing these scenes was like walking a tightwire. But I had not walked a tightwire. I had run along it, quite unconscious of any difficulty or danger. What had enabled me to do this? This is the important question, and the sole reason why I have described how I wrote the act. Any of the nonsensical scenes in, say, *The Bad Samaritan* had required far more thought and effort than this whole difficult act. Why? I shall be told that this is because one play was in my true creative vein and the other was not. But this does not take us very far. It does not explain how a number of tricky technical problems were solved at top speed and without effort. The Unconscious Mind is now brought in. I had really been pondering over this act and its problems for some time, and gradually the Unconscious somehow worked it all out and shot up the results as fast as they were needed. Something like this does happen with some pieces of work. They come easily, smoothly, because most of the work has been done during long spells of brooding. A play of mine called *Eden End* came like that. I had wandered round that Yorkshire country doctor's house for a long time. But here there had been none of this. I had started almost 'from scratch'. There had been no preliminary work in the hinterland of my mind. The Unconscious had had no time to become my Slave of the Ring on this particular job. So we must now fall back on our old fairy god-mother, Inspiration. But this is at once vague and awkward. It is awkward because even my vanity shrinks from a public claim to have been 'inspired'. It is vague because as a verb it always has an object but no subject. Who or what did the inspiring? My own explanation, which is tentative, is nearly as vague, but it does suggest a new line of enquiry.

I believe, then, that during these few hours of effortless but extremely rewarding creation, I was able, without being then aware of it, to 'tap' a reservoir of creative energy and skill, which reservoir is really the source of all so-called inspiration. Into my mind came flooding a much greater mind. Do not mistake me here. I am not claiming that a play of mine was really the work of some world-mind. This would be a monstrous impertinence. The play itself, the people and scenes in it, all these are coloured and shaped by my own ego, and exhibit all my own particular weaknesses and merits. But that triumphant rush of energy and skill, enabling me to run across the dramatic tightwire effortlessly, just for this one act, was not really my own doing, and owed its existence to the fact, which might or might not be the product of chance, that this immensely greater mind could for the time being sustain my own mind. I was indeed not so much a creator myself as an instrument of creation. Such skill as I had was a mere sharpening of the pencil that this mysterious hand might suddenly use. I have always been inclined to believe that the artist is really more of a technician and less of a genuine creator than he often pretends or is thought to be, though this may seem to contradict what I have just said about my play being my own. But what is called creative imagination seems to me not a mere by-product of the workings of the individual mind – this is probably Fancy, which might help to explain the difference between Fancy and Imagination that Coleridge and the romantics were always worrying about – but a kind of vital link between our minds and this world-mind, which may lend us its own insight into the life about us or give us glimpses of other modes of being. Again, the sudden arrival of what seems to us a wonderful idea, bringing with it a state of genuine ecstasy, may be the result of a temporary union with this greater mind. And again, when we feel exhausted and there is still much to be done, and we pray in an open selfless mood for more energy, often receiving it in a surprising measure, it sometimes seems as if we are being sustained by that greater mind. (I am well aware of the fact that every great religion the world has known observes and explains these things.) To many people, all this to-do about my Second Act will seem vague and rather pompous, yet I am sure no author, painter, musician, having known the same experience, will agree with them, or consider it a waste of time to try and pluck the heart out of this shining mystery, which occasionally irradiates the inward life of every artist.

from *Rain Upon Godshill*, 1939

FUTURE OF THE THEATRE

*THE SECOND WORLD WAR gave rise to hopes for major improve-
ments in life in this country once hostilities were ended. My father
was very active in this field, because he felt the opportunity had been
missed after the First World War, when things slipped back to the old
divisive ways. Looking for ways to improve the organisation of the
Theatre, he found a partial answer in a book* Theatre in Soviet Russia
*by Van Gyseghem. This should not be interpreted as meaning he was
either a communist or a 'fellow traveller'; he was an old-fashioned
socialist with a mind open to suggestions for a better life, whatever
their source. Narrow-minded critics preferred to attack him for assumed
political allegiance (though he was never a member of any political
party), rather than accept the sense of his views.*

The Theatre is accepted in Russia as an important social
institution, and is not regarded as a triviality, on the same
level as greyhound racing and taproom diversions. Most of
the theatres with established reputations are supported by
the State.

Each theatre is controlled by its director, whose personality
gives it its particular character. Both directors and actors are
carefully trained, have ample time allowed for rehearsal, and,
so long as they work conscientiously, may look forward to a
reasonable security. There is enormous public enthusiasm
for the Theatre.

Now, compare this with what happens here in our
commercial Theatre. Our directors and actors have no feeling
of security. Their relation with the public is often dubious
and uneasy. Too often they feel that they and their art are at
the mercy of commercial speculators who have no special
feeling for the Theatre and might just as well be manufacturing
dish-cloths or selling bicycles. All the dignity and nobility of
this ancient and communal art are squeezed out. What was

good enough for a Sophocles or a Shakespeare, a Molière or a Shaw, becomes 'show business'.

Some serious persons, probably because they have been disappointed by the triviality of the playhouse, merely shrug the topic away when you mention the Theatre to them. They imagine, I suppose, that in this age of vast transitions, when the printed word of books and the press and the spoken word of radio are so important, the Theatre is merely an old-fashioned toy, so much light entertainment for the frivolous-minded. And these people are, in my view, completely and dangerously wrong. Our present need of the compelling emotional power and the rigorous challenge of great Theatre is very strong indeed.

I happen to have worked in many of these different fields, and it is my experience that the Theatre, when it is properly handled, leaves the deepest and most satisfying impression on contemporary minds. The peculiar form of communal response that it demands (to a much higher degree than films or the radio) is very important to our time and temperament. Finally, I believe that these facts are beginning to assert themselves, that the Theatre is about to emerge here in its true shape and stature, and that therefore we do well to ask questions about its organisation.

Have we here in this Soviet system a perfect model? For some departments of theatrical organization – notably in the training and employment of actors, the methods of production, the financing of the theatres, the sale of seats – the answer could be an almost unqualified affirmative. We can start learning now from our Russian friends. But have they nothing whatever to learn from us, in this as in other things? I believe they have. In the Theatre, as in other kinds of activity, the perfect system would be about two parts Russian to one part British.

Theatres, no matter how wonderful their organization and methods, must have plays to produce, and, in my view, if those theatres are to remain vital, they must have contemporary plays to produce and not be content to play tricks with old masterpieces. And it cannot be denied, except by political propagandists, who are ready to deny any inconvenient fact, that all this wonderful theatrical activity in Russia, from which we can learn so much, has been strangely disappointing in the quality of dramatic writing it has produced.

The old Russia, which nobody in his senses regrets, gave us Gogol, Ostrovsky, Tolstoy, Chekhov, Gorki, Andreyev – to name no others. If there is anybody of this quality writing for the Soviet Theatre, then let his work be translated and shown to us at once, because all the volumes I have waded through so far have been of a very different quality. And I suspect there is a good reason for this.

The dramatist in Russia has many advantages that we dramatists here may well envy. He has innumerable fine companies waiting for his work, and gigantic audiences ready to applaud it. He is comparatively better rewarded, not only in money and what it will buy, but also in public prestige, than we are here. But we have one advantage that may easily outweigh all of his. We are free to develop in our own way as artists.

Let us walk carefully here. I am not now declaring that art demands seclusion in an ivory tower, or that an artist should not deal with public questions and social problems, or anything of the sort. Indeed, I happen to believe that a dramatist in our time will work best if he should find himself excited and inspired by the great social and political issues of the time. (If only because he will find an eager response in the minds of his audience.) But – and here's the point – he must be privately excited and inspired, and not dictated to by a committee.

Furthermore, the criticism he receives should not be too narrowly political and official. The critics should have a certain freedom of response just as the artist should have freedom to create. Dramatic criticism here tends to be too personal, rather old-fashioned in its indifference to wide social issues, out of touch with the times, but from the little I have seen of Soviet theatrical criticism (chiefly notices of my own plays there), clearly it goes to the other extreme, and reads as if it were dictated by the heads of a government department to their public relations officer.

Now, art is a kind of public relations, but in an altogether more plastic and subtler form than this. Clamp the artists into a system like this, and you immediately limit his growth as an artist. This, I believe, has happened in Soviet Russia, which has the most magnificent Theatre in the world, but still awaits its great dramatists.

John O'London's Weekly, 24 September 1943

Later that year he wrote a thorough appraisal of the Theatre in mid war, and prospects for the future.

Already there are signs that the Theatre in this country will come out of the war in a stronger position than it has ever enjoyed before, and that post-war developments may be very impressive indeed. Here is some of the evidence. First, in spite of raids, black-out and transport difficulties, the extraordinary activity of the Theatre in the West End. A good deal of rubbish is produced and lavishly supported, but the general level of entertainment in London is at least equal to that of pre-war years. In the larger provincial theatres, the standard is probably rather higher and the audiences are certainly greater than before the war. The repertory theatres are carrying on in most places, and often playing to capacity. Amateur dramatic companies are suffering, of course, from lack of man-power, but some of the best of them – such as the Bradford Civic – are still doing excellent work.

CEMA in the factory hostels and small towns and villages and ENSA in the camps are now introducing large numbers of young men and women to the Drama, and so are in fact creating new audiences for the Theatre. The response, especially in the hostels, is eager and enthusiastic. These young workers like the Theatre. Players report that these new audiences are stimulating. I do not believe that after the war all these people will be content with radio and an occasional visit to the cinema. They will demand their share of the living Theatre.

The post-war Theatre should be organised on a national basis and must no longer be a welter of competing interests. Its structure, on this national basis, can be seen as a pyramid. At the apex dominating and inspiring the whole dramatic effort, should be several absolutely first-class professional companies that have not been created to make money for anybody and are as remote from commercial interests as the National Gallery. Their job would be to show people what the Theatre can do as its best. I believe that these companies, which would play both in London and the larger provincial cities, would soon pay handsomely, but – and this is a very important but – they would not have been organised simply to produce a profit. They represent the nation expressing itself in drama under the best possible conditions. They should be subsidised nationally. If it is proposed to continue the Entertainment Tax, then some of the money this Tax produces should be returned to the Theatre by way of subsidising these special companies. And this is merely feeding the goose that lays the golden eggs.

Every town of any size should have its theatre, just as it has its schools and libraries. If private enterprise cannot build a theatre, then public enterprise should do it. Some people, of course, do not want to go to theatres, but then lots of people (I am one of them) do not want to play bowls or go boating in public parks. What elderly rate-payers should be made to understand is that a theatre is just as essential an amenity as a park or a library. Moreover, these theatres will very soon pay for themselves. But even if they have to be heavily subsidised at first that is no reason for not creating them. A great many people need the drama nowadays. It relieves the strain of close hard work and changing conditions. It brings people colour and wit, laughter, tears, and insight. And because it is essentially communal, it strengthens the feeling of commun-ity. An audience has to play a part – really the most important part – in a theatrical performance, and playing this part in a satisfying performance does the members of an audience a world of good. Politicians rarely understand this, and so rarely support the Theatre, simply because they themselves are always busy acting in the drama at Westminster. It is high time they realised that most people have not their advantages. As for Town Councils, they should not be filled with elderly men whose chief desire is to keep the rates down and then go home and have a nap.

Many of these municipal theatres will, of course, have their repertory companies. I hope, however, that it will be possible to organise these repertory companies in groups so that instead of 'Weekly Rep', which is a horror of under-rehearsal and overwork, they have productions that last for several weeks by touring the little local circuit of repertory theatres. Again, the local amateur dramatic societies, instead of competing and quarrelling with the repertory people, should work with them, occasionally borrowing personnel and often seeking advice. This inter-relation of theatrical enterprise, professional and amateur, appears to be well-managed in Russia. We stand very much in need here of this careful organisation and very useful overlapping in our drama. When you climb the Great

Pyramid at Gizeh you have to be hoisted up every step, and we need far more of this hoisting up in the pyramid of our national Theatre. In the past I have often visited provincial towns where there were plenty of people interested in the Theatre, but unfortunately they were all busy competing instead of co-operating.

I am myself very strongly in favour of well-equipped drama departments attached to our universities, as they are in America. The great progress made in America during the last 25 years, in dramatic writing, production, acting, has been largely the work, in my view, of these dramatic schools. There is much, of course, that cannot be taught, but the very fact that young men and women are given the opportunity to write, act, produce, design and paint scenery, play about with lighting, means that they gain most valuable experience. In addition to these permanent dramatic schools, there should be plenty of special short courses, summer schools and the like, in every branch of theatrical activity. Here, perhaps to the astonishment of some readers, I include writing. Now it is obvious that no amount of instruction can produce a dramatist. Imagination, observation, invention, cannot be taught. Either you have them or you have not. But that does not mean that nothing can be taught. During the last ten years I have seen many plays by new writers in which the dramatic material was excellent but the handling of the material, the general construction, was so deplorable that the plays failed disastrously; and I believe that the writers of these plays, who had genuine gifts, would have gained enormously by some almost elementary instruction and perhaps, in addition, some theatrical experience that might easily be obtained even in a summer school. I suggest too that young writers and producers of notable promise should be given scholarships, preferably sufficiently generous to enable them to travel.

What has been chiefly wrong with our Theatre up to now – and I see many signs of improvement – has been that nearly everybody concerned with it has had the wrong attitude of mind. Thus, successful dramatists, producers and actors have been content to enjoy their success without reference to the general condition of the Theatre. They have tended to take the self-made man's line of, 'What was good enough for me ought to be good enough for you.' Then managers, instead of deliberately adopting a policy and trying to organise their part of the Theatre, have too often regarded the West End as simply another Monte Carlo. They have been, in fact, gamblers not managers. Then again, provincial theatrical people have too often been waiting for some lucky break that would land them into Shaftesbuy Avenue, instead of making up their minds to turn their own Coketown into the theatrical capital of the country. Again, a great many amateur producers and players only think of themselves as the dashing rivals of the professionals and never see themselves as humble contributors to a great communal art. Finally, both the press and the public would help by dropping this 'Let's go to a show' kind of talk, which always belonged to Broadway rather than Britain and is, in my view, an enemy of the serious Theatre.

This does not mean that we should all become priggish about the Theatre. God forbid that we should turn it into a temple of boredom. Let us have honest entertainment indeed. But let it be entertainment worthy of the time and of the people who are struggling so heroically in this time, and presented not in a hotchpotch of shabby halls run meanly for easy profit but in a great national institution.

The Author, Winter 1943

LETTER TO A THEATRE OWNER

WHAT IS IT that, year in and year out, keeps the Theatre going, and enables you people to pay your rents, rates and wages? It is first a supply of good new plays, which will generally be the work of professional dramatists. Secondly, it is a supply of leading actors and actresses whose names and ability are known to the play-going public. (I am not now saying how things ought to be, I am telling you how they are.) With some experienced and hard-working professional dramatists, continually bringing something new into the playhouse, and plenty of capable and well-known leading actors and actresses, the Theatre can carry on, and the playhouses – your playhouses, mark you – will never be empty.

If these dramatists and players are already making their reputations, then the Theatre in five years' time will be safe.

You ought to have been ready to lose money (though the loss would never have been felt) in order to create new dramatists and new leading players, to make sure of your future audiences. Instead of that, you have often deliberately kept out of your theatres the very productions that would establish new reputations, which would ultimately benefit you more than anybody.

PS. If it comes to a pinch, what with books, films and radio, we writers can do without theatres, you know. But can theatre owners?

'Letter to a Theatre Owner', *New Theatre*, June 1946

MOMENT DURING REHEARSAL

MANY PLAYWRIGHTS enjoy attending performances of their own plays. Night after night will find them lurking at the back of the dress circle, and if they are discovered and challenged there they will pretend to be keeping an eye on old Brown, who plays the doctor, or deciding whether there could be a cut toward the end of Act Two. But – bless their hearts – they are really there to enjoy themselves. Now I am not one of these playwrights. Once a play is running smoothly I try to stay away from it. One reason is that I have given the production so much close study during the rehearsal period and have watched so carefully the first performances that I am weary of the piece and want to think about something else. If it is a serious play, I am more likely to be irritated than moved by it. If it is a comedy, then the sight and sound of the audience laughing do not make me think what a fine funny fellow I am, but arouse in me feelings of disgust. So there is no delight here for me. That comes much earlier, at some point during rehearsal. After the preliminary readings, which are interesting rather than delightful, you struggle along with moves and 'business', and the actors put aside their scripts and try to remember their words; and all this for the author is rather like conducting a party of tourists across fields of glue. But then, if you are lucky, there comes a moment when – suddenly, miraculously – the play is alive. There is no set, no lights, no costumes and make-up, no effects, no audience, yet perhaps the play is more alive than it will ever be again for you. You forget that you are still messing about with chairs and orange-boxes and chalklines on an empty stage lit with one glaring bulb. You forget the cleaners still chattering and banging in the upper circle, and the empties that are being noisily taken out of the stalls bar. You forget the traffic roaring outside. You forget that this theatre has merely been lent to you until five o'clock, and that as yet you have no theatre of your own. You forget all these things because now a miracle happens. The stage manager and his assistant, seated at their familiar table, marking the prompt script, fade from your consciousness. The horrible 'working light' is no longer there; strange dawns and exquisite sunsets appear. The chalklines and orange-boxes turn into walls and tables and sofas, all perfect. Miss Thing, wearing her oldest clothes, her hair anyhow, with pinched features and a yellow complexion, suddenly transforms herself into the beautiful creature of your imagination. Young So-and-so – up to now a lout and a bad bit of casting – flashingly emerges as a gay and handsome breaker of hearts. Old Whose-it, who seemed to be a mistake, if only because he drinks too much and cannot remember a line, is now your lovable Old Smith to the last wrinkle and chuckle. And what pathos – what comedy – what suspense – what truth to life – what profound symbolism! Yes, it is here – as you first imagined it – no, better – much better – oh glory! Only for a few minutes at best; but while it lasts, this transfiguration, what delight!

from *Delight 16*

PROGRESS IN THE THEATRE

SOMETIMES it seemed that to be in the auditorium, staring at the closed curtain, eagerly anticipating the performance, provided a special magic. My father regretted the demise of the curtain in the modern Theatre:

It may be true, as younger directors tell us, that by abolishing the prosceniums and their curtains, by using a stage projecting well into the audience, productions can be both more intimate and more economical. But it should be recognised that a good deal has been lost. (The perfect theatre would be able to use the projecting open stage and, when necessary, the proscenium and curtain.) To begin with, there is something unsatisfactory, to my mind, about going into a theatre and having to look at ghostly tables and chairs, rocks and trees, there on the darkened open stage. Again, there is a loss of dramatic effect at the end of each act when no curtain is being used. The descent of the curtain, all the time I was writing plays, was no mere mechanical process, any more than the acting and lighting were. We writers, if we knew our business, indicated the Curtain speed we wanted, ranging from a Very Slow, creeping down and almost like a sigh to end the scene, to a Fast Curtain, like a brutal shout at such goings-on; and if we had any sense we were on hand when these various Curtains were rehearsed. Perhaps more important still is the loss of that magic which belonged to the curtain, raised to give you your first sight of the other world of the play, lowered to return you to your own world.

Moreover, when the open curtainless stage arrived, the footlights had to go. These, called 'floats' in Britain and 'foots' in America, worked notable magic. (I seem to be writing now for the young.) They came up as the house lights went down, illuminating the lower folds of the curtain, as if a sunlight we had never quite known were arriving in this other world. Again they fought the drastic top-lighting that threatens actresses' good looks. Finally, we not only varied the colours of the 'floats' but also planted among them tiny 'baby spots' that would stealthily illuminate a little table or a single chair. And now at a time when provincial theatres may be turned into bingo halls, surely there is something to be said for restoring some of the old magic? We don't have to be disenchanted out of everything.

Outcries and Asides, 1974

FINANCE

MY FATHER was always interested in the practicalities of making Theatre available. Even before there were subsidised theatres he encouraged reduced prices to open theatres to a wider audience; he was a partner in the Mask Theatre set up for this very purpose. His play Johnson Over Jordan *had played to near capacity in the cheaper seats but little business for the more expensive seats, so he boldly cut all the prices.*

Cutprice Theatre

I have just concluded arrangements to present no fewer than three productions in the West End at less than standard Theatre prices. First, with Mr Basil Dean, I am transferring my new play, *Johnson Over Jordan*, to the Saville at reduced prices. Then, with my old associate, Mr J P Mitchelhill, I am bringing my Yorkshire comedy, *When We Are Married*, which ran for over 200 performances at ordinary prices, into the Prince's Theatre, where we shall open at half-prices. And later in the same week we hope to present Shaw's *Doctor's Dilemma* at the Whitehall Theatre, also at half-prices.

What is the idea behind this policy? Is it simply trying to get through a dead theatrical season by running at bargain prices? Is it the equivalent of a shop's annual clearance sale? No, it is not. My friends and I are cutting prices in the Theatre in order to give the Theatre new life. We are like gardeners pruning a tree.

The whole Theatre must not be made dependent upon people who really only want light entertainment. If it is, then it will be impossible for serious dramatists, who demand some intelligence from their audiences, to exist at all.

There is another and fairly large class of people composed of those who can appreciate real dramatic art, but have almost ceased going to West End theatres because they dislike paying out good money for poor stuff. They will tell you that they have been taken in too often. It is urgently necessary – for those of us who write serious plays – that these people be brought into the Theatre. We can do it not only by offering them productions that are not an insult to their intelligence, but also by offering them comfortable seats at reduced prices.

Then again there are masses and masses of people who are clean outside the playgoing habit. They have grown up with cinemas not theatres. Bring them into the Theatre and they will enjoy it enormously. The film has magic, but the play has still more magic. There is an enormous public waiting to go to the Theatre.

It must not be imagined that we are able now to cut prices because previously our margin of profit was enormous. It was not. We can only succeed with these new prices if our expenses are cut down too.

Once we have consistent policies, more economical producing, actors under long contract at reasonable salaries, then, if the public will only stand by us, we can go ahead and give our fellow citizens a first-class Theatre at prices to suit everybody. All we ask is a little loyalty, co-operation, a communal feeling for what is a communal art.

Sunday Pictorial, 19 March 1939

Tax and the Theatre

Throughout his life my father had trenchant views on tax; he was not against tax as such, realising that public services had to be paid for, but, as with most things, he insisted on a system that was fair and reasonable. Certain taxes he felt were poorly thought out and did not respect the particular circumstances of the taxpayer. For instance he complained long and loud about the burden of surtax on authors who often had to pay as much as 95 per cent of their income in tax in a good year, with little allowance for the many lean years that might have preceded it. In the 1930s all places of entertainment were liable to levy Entertainment Tax on the price of entry. The funds raised went into the general exchequer; he found this unreasonable.

I am thinking of asking the Treasury to finance my next theatrical production. This is not unreasonable. If I keep my theatre dark, the State makes nothing out of me, but if I summon up enough courage and capital to put on a play, and the play fills the theatre every night, then the State makes about £250 a week out of us in Entertainment Tax, and afterwards slices off about a third of all our profits. If we lose our money, then of course the State has not been a partner in the gamble. If no theatrical gamblers could be found, if all the theatres in London were dark, the State would not only find itself with a dismal chief city, unattractive to visitors (who spend money and can be taxed), but would also lose a substantial revenue in Entertainment Tax. Yet not a penny of public money is spent on the Theatre.

I have lately acquired the West End rights of a play that seems to me a work of genius, in its own way just as much a work of genius as any of the pictures so carefully housed and lit in our public galleries. When I can find the right theatre for this play I shall produce it there, and hope and hope that it will not take every penny of the necessarily modest sum I am prepared to lose on it. The State has no interest in this matter. It will, however, the moment people come and see the play. It will take care that they are soundly taxed for their idiotic extravagance. Meanwhile, I am foolish enough to think that the production of a play of such merit is an act of public service.

This is not the customary plea for the removal of the Entertainment Tax. If things are going well, the Theatre and its patrons can afford to pay this tax. I am for letting the tax stand. It is time, however, that the State regarded the Theatre as something more than a fruitful source of revenue. You do not keep milking a cow without feeding it. The State should return some of this revenue to its source, and that source is the serious Theatre.

I do not propose to define the serious Theatre, beyond saying that it is the Theatre run by sensible cultivated persons for other sensible cultivated persons. It is, in fact, any Theatre served with passion, intelligence and integrity. Now this Theatre has to struggle for its very existence. It loses more money that it gains. Authors, actors, producers, backers are continually making self-sacrifices for it. They bring to it money they earn elsewhere. There is no reason why the State should not return a portion of what it takes from dramatic entertainment to what I believe to be the inspirational source of that entertainment, the serious Theatre. We are entitled to a dividend on that enormous revenue. It could restore the Theatre in the provinces. It could provide serious amateur dramatic societies with professional producers. It could help to finance interesting productions. It could provide the necessary financial backing to enable groups of young players, now trailing round the agents' offices here in London, to form themselves into touring companies for the smaller towns. It could give scholarships to young dramatists and producers of exceptional promise. It could do all this and more by returning to audiences a shilling [five pence] for every pound it has taken out of their pockets. There would still be 19 shillings [95 pence] left to spend on aeroplanes and battleships and the vast explorings of avenues.

The New Statesman and Nation, 17 November 1934

He returned to the attack in 1937:

I write novels and I produce plays, and to me the plays are every bit as important as the novels. But when I publish a novel the people who buy it do not pay anything to the Government. In deed, a certain amount of public money is spent buying copies of the novel.

During the last few years, the Government has taken millions of pounds in Entertainment Tax, chiefly, of course, from films. But films owe an immense debt to the serious Theatre, which has supplied them with players, directors, writers, story material. But this same serious Theatre is being run at a loss, is fighting for its very existence, and is working against every possible disadvantage, including crippling taxation. Probably our politicians think the Theatre is nothing better than an idle show because they live near the West End, where there are few real plays and a great many 'shows'.

Yet the interest in dramatic art is not leaving us. The Theatre is not falling down, as some people appear to think. There is something in modern life, especially in our great industrial areas, that asks for release in drama. The result is that there are more and more Repertory, Civic, Little Theatres, and more and more amateur dramatic societies. We are as a people more Theatre-minded than we ever were before.

And it must not be forgotten that the Theatre is a lavish employer. In full swing it can use the services of thousands of players, musicians, scene-painters, carpenters, electricians and attendants. And all these people are here, on the spot, and are not being employed six thousand miles away in Hollywood. For this reason alone, quite apart from cultural considerations, the Theatre deserves preferential treatment in the matter of taxation. Why tax people out of employment? Wages and good drama are better than unemployment and doles. We have many things to fight – the growth of mechanical entertainment, increased rents, wages, general costs, the growing triviality of West End taste – and it is hopeless when we still have our hands tied by taxes.

News Chronicle, 29 July 1937

THE ARTS UNDER SOCIALISM

IT IS ALWAYS an honour to address the Fabian Society. Even I realise that, although I thoroughly dislike the business of lecturing and have almost a horror of lecture audiences, though their eyes may shine with Fabian intelligence and goodwill. I realise too, that I am specially honoured by being allowed to take part in this particular series of lectures, which worthily celebrates your long and triumphant career as a society by offering you important talks by immense Labour Party bigwigs, men of high office, prestige and influence, in whose company I cut a rather poor figure. On the other hand, the subject I have been given is practically a death trap. Politicians and editors and other experienced hands run from it screaming. I may be wrong about your eyes shining with intelligence and goodwill; they may be glittering with sinister anticipation; but I dare not stop to make sure. However, before plunging into the middle of my subject, which is The Artist in a Socialist State, I must point out that from now on when I speak of art or the arts I do not mean merely the visual arts, painting and the like, but all the various arts; that when I refer to artists I mean the creators and executants in all these arts; and that when I say 'the State' I am referring to the political organisation of a national society and not to the community itself, the total of all its individuals.

Let me begin by declaring firmly that, in my view, the Socialist State exists for the artists, and not the artists for the State.

Naturally I do not mean that the State exists for the artists alone, although I have known artists who would be prepared to tell you so. But what I am affirming is that the creation and appreciation of the arts – or let us call all this simply art – is one of the ends towards which the Socialist State is the means. This does not imply art for art's sake. There is no such thing as art for art's sake; there is only pottering and playing about for pottering and playing about's sake. Real art would blow that little pigeon-hole to smithereens in a second. But we must get our values right.

The State, as distinct from the community, is a form of organisation, really a piece of machinery. The creation and the true appreciation of art are spiritual activities. It would be monstrous to suggest, though it has been done before now, that spiritual activities exist to serve a piece of machinery. So, I repeat, the State exists for the artists, and not the artists for the State.

Nature of Art and Artists

The commonest mistake made about art is to assume that it is like the icing on a cake. Nearly all politicians take to this error as a duck takes to water. I am not blaming them: they have been thoroughly conditioned by their strange habits, outlook and mode of life. All of these encourage them to believe that art is like the icing on the substantial cake of ordinary sensible living, is like the bits of decoration, usually atrocious, that are added to a large public building, is like the coffee-brandy-and-cigars that round off a thundering good dinner; that the artist is the clever but vague chap you call in after the serious work of the day has been done, to help your digestion, to add a bit of fancywork that the ladies – God bless 'em – will appreciate, to pass the time in the long winter evenings. (And just imagine asking Michelangelo, Shakespeare, Rembrandt, Beethoven and similar giants to pop in for the evening on those terms.) I need hardly add here that this has been very much the view of art and the artists preferred in capitalist societies, whose leaders are often secretly terrified of the passion and insight, the vast generosity and searching vision of the great artists. But unfortunately, many Socialists, though they may pay a lip-service to Art, think along the same lines, a fact that ought to have warned them that something was wrong.

Two or three months ago, in a Tory propaganda sheet, a certain Brutus, whose style no longer resembled Shakespeare's but had dwindled to one uncommonly like Mr Beverley Baxter's, rebuked me at the top of his voice for suggesting that the people of this country might forget some of their material scarcities, might work harder and more cheerfully, might get a great lift at a time when they needed it, if they were offered a far more generous dose of the arts, with all the colour, wit, insight and vision they could bring. This Brutus told me that all the people of this country wanted were more greyhound tracks, race meetings and football matches and the like, and never mind about art. Now, oddly enough, I feel that this Brutus really understood art better than many of our Socialist friends, and that, understanding it, he did not particularly want the people to have it. And why? Because art is not really like the icing on the cake, it is far more like the yeast in the dough. It is not something added, for decoration and fancy-work, when the solid job has been done; it is much nearer the leaven, permeating and then aerating and lifting the doughy stuff of life. The true artist is not some vague fiddling chap on the edge of things: he is the man who is staring harder, seeing and remembering more, feeling more keenly, getting closer to reality, and using up more vital energy, than other men are. Compared with him, most of them are half-asleep and half-dead. His response to life is altogether quicker, wider and deeper than theirs.

And when we have understood him, he has immensely enriched our lives, sharpening our eyes and ears, broadening our sympathies, quickening our imagination, and enlarging our experience. And never did men need the artist more than they do today.

In certain limited conditions life without art may be sound and healthy enough. Men who have a deep unconscious relation with nature, men who live simply and in the open, and perhaps face constant danger and make great use of their primitive instincts, can probably do without art, although they often turn instinctively to one of the simpler arts and show natural good taste in it. Thus the Americans in the pioneering stage, the men and women who opened the West, who knew and cared little about art, lived full and happy lives, and were mostly admirable types. But the modern American, living as most of us do, in great urban industrial communities, on an educated or semi-educated level, rejects art to his own danger. In these conditions, characteristic of modern Western man, life without art is life already turning sour.

Something must take the place of that leaven, and that something may be acid and corrosive. The spirit, robbed of its proper nourishment, and so hungry and frustrated, may find itself at the mercy of the dark forces of the Unconscious, and may welcome perversion, violence, cruelty and death. It is significant that the peoples who gave themselves to Fascism, even in countries that had fine artistic traditions, abruptly stopped producing art of any consequence. Something had gone wrong. And it can still go wrong elsewhere. The Socialist State, then, will do well not to undervalue and neglect its art and artists. It must try to cherish them.

Now here, as a Socialist addressing a Socialist audience, I will pay you the compliment of being perfectly frank on one point. It is this. The artist tends to be afraid of Socialism, and feels that he may be called upon to sacrifice too much for it. Do not misunderstand me. The artist in his capacity as a private citizen is more likely than not to be sympathetic towards the Left, if only because he usually has wide and generous sympathies, is free from many bourgeois prejudices, and dislikes mean, greedy, predatory types; all of which explains why at the present time the Left has far more genuine talent on its side than the Right.

But the artist *qua* artist cannot help feeling suspicious and rather gloomy about a Socialist society, and this is particularly true of the more romantic artists, who feel in their heart of hearts that they too, like Titian and others, ought to live like princes. The artist wonders rather dubiously about the Socialist atmosphere of co-operation, committees and common sense; asks himself how he will like it when splendid wealthy patrons are replaced by earnest and dreary town councillors; he is doubtful about a society that no longer has either magnificent palaces or picturesque hovels but only nice bungalows and tidy communal flats; and he is ready, secretly perhaps, to regret the dramatic values that will disappear from a society abolishing all terrific social inequalities. (Notice how Shakespeare, with all his kings and barons, clowns and shepherds, concentrated upon these inequalities, as he did too upon wildly romantic settings, to the complete neglect, in his case, of his own contemporary scene.) You will retort at once, in your sharp Fabian way, that you do not propose to relinquish the quest for social justice and to allow our society to continue looking like a dog fight, merely to flatter the romantic dreams or ease the professional tasks of artists. And the artist, nine times out of ten, will agree with you at once, but he will feel rather wistful, a trifle gloomy, not too happy about the future.

He cannot help feeling that he may be called upon, in his capacity as an artist, to sacrifice too much for this Socialism. He is ready to reject the devil of commercial exploitation but cannot look forward to the deep sea of Arts Councils and committees. Do not make haste to blame him, for he has his own private demon to satisfy, his own terribly difficult tasks to perform, and must of necessity, to get the job done, be something of an individualist and an anarchist. Be patient with him, and then he will be magnificently generous with you. When I was in the Soviet Union several people told me that the actors there were the spoilt pets of the Government. But with what a glorious result – for I never saw such acting before! And that is how it is apt to be with the artist. Offer him, and sourly too, perhaps, the barest justice, and he will give you nothing in return. Spoil him a little, and he will run to offer you the wealth of his heart and mind.

Some Necessary Conditions

All this suggests that I believe that the Socialist State should try to recompense the artist for what he may feel he has lost.

And indeed I do believe this, with certain modifications that I will indicate later, but first I will tell you what I think the State must do to achieve merely a sensible just relationship with its artists. To begin with, if the State wants plenty of good art, it must create favourable conditions for the artist. Thus, to take obvious examples, authors will feel frustrated unless the State produces adequate supplies of paper, encourages good publishing, printing and binding establishments, and provides its towns with excellent bookshops. The musicians will need plenty of good concert halls and opera houses and fine orchestras and well-trained instrumentalists and singers. The dramatists and actors and ballet dancers cannot function properly without numerous well-equipped playhouses and theatrical organisations on both a national and municipal scale. The painters and their like need a large and not too expensive supply of their special materials and implements, together with studios, galleries and shops for their particular art.

Now all this, I realise, is elementary, the dreariest common sense, to which no doubt you did not come here to listen, but I must point out that here and now, in this tentative sketch of a Socialist society of ours, not only are these elementary needs not being fulfilled but I for one know of no plans even aiming at their fulfilment in the future. We are by no means devoid of art here and our recent progress in the communal arts of music, ballet, drama, has been considerable and astonishing – but I declare without hesitation, as one still bleeding from the battle, that every bit of art we manage to achieve is almost a miracle. Artists of every kind are faced with a nightmare obstacle race, and this is not simply because of the transition from a wartime to a peacetime economy and production, in a half-ruined world, for this we can all understand; but it is also because there are too many people in authority here who fail to appreciate the importance of art in a society like ours, do not realise what a lift it can give to the spirit, and cannot understand that it may have some connection with the problems they are finding it so hard to solve. Remember that many of us have travelled recently in countries far worse off than this, and have found there that more has been done for art and the artists already than has even been dreamt of here. And so when I offer you an elementary and obvious sketch of conditions absolutely necessary to the artist, conditions that must be the responsibility of any State that has a planned economy, do not blame me and yawn in my face, for I tell you that we are not within the remotest sight of such conditions here in Britain.

On the other hand, we are still walled in with conditions of another kind that the Socialist State must promptly abolish. The artist is easily exploited, partly because his mind is not conditioned to hard bargaining, and partly too because he is apt to imagine that he is tougher and craftier in the ways of this world than he actually is. (This is one of the favourite illusions of many simple and kindly souls, of whom Arnold Bennett was a notable example.)

It is the duty of the Socialist State to protect its artists from exploitation as it is to protect its householders from burglary.

I do not say that the State alone should do this, for I am in favour of artists of every sort forming strong professional associations and unions that will do this too. Many such associations and unions already exist, but in my view they should have more power and make more use of it, not only making sure that their members are not being exploited but also looking after their interests in every possible way. But artists are notoriously bad joiners and committee men – and some of the best of them feel compelled to walk alone – and therefore I say that the State must be ready to protect them against exploitation. On the other hand, it is to be hoped that in a socialist society the number of pirates, brigands, vampires and leeches will be severely reduced, and that expensive parasites and hangers-on to the arts will be asked to justify their existence, with strong hints given of useful work waiting to be done elsewhere. All this may seem obvious enough, but this point about exploitation is worth making, especially in view of what follows.

Though the state itself should be a generous patron of artists of many kinds, I do not believe that it should maintain its artists so long as they are able to work and to keep themselves. All that the state should do is to create the conditions most favourable for the self-maintenance of artists. I am against any proposed system that would turn artists who are neither ill nor old into civil servants or state pensioners. It is true that many artists of considerable reputation long for security, and that this security could easily be bought by a regular state salary, with the state repaying itself by claiming whatever the work of such artists might earn. There is nothing difficult about this, and something of the kind, in more than one art, was almost achieved during the war. But in my view this security would be bought by both the artist and the public at a heavy price, and there are several good reasons for not adopting such a system. The first is, that so long as exploitation is barred the relation of patron-artist is healthy and good for both the artists and the public. The latter like to feel that by their own direct patronage they are expressing their admiration of and gratitude for the artist's work. It gives them too a certain responsibility about it. I for one do not want a society in which art is laid on like hot and cold water. If people are earning good money, then they should be ready to pay good money for what they enjoy. One day, perhaps, when a generation has grown up in a true Socialist atmosphere, the general attitude may be quite different, but as people are at present and will be in the near future, they tend to undervalue what is given away for nothing or for very little. And if they genuinely like something, they are glad to pay for it – and to feel they are helping to reward its creator. As for the artist – although there may be some exceptions to this – as a rule he enjoys this direct patron relationship with his public, cheerfully accepts the fact that his professional life is more of a gamble than most people's lives are, and would rather take his chance, especially in a society in which people have leisure and some money to spend on it, than be placed by the state on a salary list – and that is even if he agreed, as most artists would certainly not agree, that his position on that salary list was as high as his own reputation.

Control of Copyright

But that is only the beginning. If we ask the state to maintain its artists, it will soon want to exercise two different kinds of control, both of which are bad. First, it will want to own the copyright of the artist's work, as it did in many instances during the war. (I insisted upon taking my name off a booklet I wrote about one Government Department during the war, because the text had been mutilated after it left my hands.)

Now it is very important indeed that the artist should own the copyright of his own work and thus be able to exercise a thorough control over what happens to that work. I am not thinking now in terms of financial rewards at all; nor really making concessions to the artist's individualism. It is important from the public's point of view too. A work of art is a very personal and intimate creation, an expression at once elaborate and delicate of the mind of the artist, a thing that might take years to make and yet be ruined in five minutes; and this being the case, then clearly it is only wise to leave the artist more or less in charge of the destiny of his work.

It is he who knows best about it, has most at stake in the matter, and therefore, if only to prevent the work from being knocked about to suit anybody's convenience, we must strengthen his control by the full force of the laws of copyright. Any other move with some public department taking charge, might easily be fatal to the work of art as a work of art. By agreeing to this, not only are we pleasing and encouraging the artists, but we the public are protecting ourselves from all manner of ruinous processes, editing, cutting, bowdlerising, and mischievous or idle tinkering.

Allow me to give you a personal instance. During the last 18 months, various plays of mine have been and are being performed all over Europe, where I have seen many of them, mostly with pleasure. But not long ago, in a city still with an Allied Commission, I found in one theatre a play of mine being performed in a mutilated shape, to suit the temporary policy of this particular theatre. Now this had happened because neither myself nor my agent had been able to negotiate directly with this theatre, because a public department was left to do the job in that city. Here the copyright, and therefore the control, was temporarily out of my hands – with a lamentable result, new in my experience. It is only fair to add that the officials concerned echoed my terrible outcries, once

I pointed out to them what was happening to my play; but some mischief had already been done, and if I had not chanced to visit that city, it would have continued. And that is merely a tiny instance of what would happen on a gigantic scale if the fate of works of art was no longer the direct concern of their creators but was left in charge of public officials. Incidentally, our present law, which allows copyright to lapse after a sufficient interval, is sensible enough: by that time the work has existed so long that the way in which the artist left it is well known, and presumably he has been rewarded sufficiently for creating it. But why these sensible rules should be applied to literary property and not to some other – and far less personal – kinds, has always been a mystery to my simple mind.

Danger of Committee Art

Then there is another kind of control that the State would soon begin to exercise if it were responsible for maintaining its artists. It would remind them that he who pays the piper calls the tune. It would begin to dictate what kind of art these State servants must produce. Why should good public money be paid out for mysterious fancy stuff that hardly anybody understands?

You can hear the Questions in the House, and the 'Hear, hear, hear!' greeting the apologetic Minister who promised that something was about to be done to prevent any further public funds being wasted in this fashion. A controlling authority would soon be created, and this would consist of politicians and busybodies, who would probably know nothing about art, or of elderly artistic bigwigs, academic types, who would know so much about art that any flash of original genius would set them in a rage. We should then be worse off than we have been in the past. A dull mediocrity would flourish, and the chances of great art, vital, original, inspiring, would be sadly reduced. And I hope everybody here will agree with me when I declare that we have not brought Socialism into this world in order to keep great art out of it. It is somewhere here that we part company with our Communist friends, with whom I seem to have debated this issue recently in many different parts of Europe. We jog along finely together for a good part of the way, but then suddenly arrive at a crossroads. As I hesitate, they are bewildered and saddened by my sudden revelation of unsuspected bourgeois prejudices, the lingering traces in me of decadent Liberalism, idealism, mysticism, and my astonishing ignorance of dialectical materialism, Socialist realism, and sound Communism. And I on my part point out that no central committee of any party, though its members plan and toil for the people night after night until their eyes are bloodshot, is fit to tell artists what they should do and how they should do it. The good writer, I tell them, is by reason of his imagination and insight looking further ahead than the politician and the official, and therefore should not be lingering in the rear of them, waiting for orders. Just as central committees probably do not want any real art, which they might easily find too disturbing, so too the rest of us do not want Central Committee art, including all those huge bad pictures of the chairman decorating the secretary with the Order of the Golden Hammer. Let the committees get on with their job, and the artists with theirs. And if you tell me that I am now disposing of a very important issue – and I admit its extreme importance, and I know that it is haunting many of our minds these days – much too briefly and flippantly, I shall agree; but I hope to return to it later. What I am still arguing here is that it is dangerous for the State to maintain its artists, instead of merely doing its best, which it is there to do, to ensure the conditions that will enable the artists to proceed with their tasks and to keep themselves. For, I repeat, the price is too high.

Problem of the Original Genius

Now, before tackling one or two difficulties, I must add a note of criticism. During the last 20 years, I have noticed, there seems to have been a good deal of confusion, which has addled the minds of many critics, between the popular and mixed arts, like that of the novelist or the dramatist, and the pure and highly technical arts of the musician or the painter. I will separate them at once by declaring that I know no instance of a great novelist or dramatist who was not reasonably popular and whose work was not fairly well understood and appreciated in his own lifetime; whereas with the highly original composer or painter, who may have had to create the very tradition by which his work can be understood or appreciated, who may have demanded that the listener or spectator should unlearn one set of technical values, while learning another quite new set, there may be a sad timelag, and he may go to his grave long before he could collect an audience large enough to supply him with the bare necessities of life. And clearly it is these geniuses, often of marvellous achievement and influence, who present us with our hardest problems. For example, some years ago I read a book on politics and culture by an extreme Left Winger, enthusiastic but rather slapdash; and among the examples he gave of fine original geniuses who suffered under stupid capitalism was Cezanne. Now we have no time tonight for art criticism, so let us all agree, as I most certainly do, that Cezanne was a great painter – and also a most powerful influence – who was not appreciated during his lifetime. Probably the smallest of his sketches would now fetch more than the sum total he made out of his pictures while he lived. But unfortunately our friend, the extreme Left Winger, in his cultural attack upon capitalism, could hardly have found a worse example to support him than Cezanne. For what was it that enabled this strange solitary genius to conduct his experiments, year after year, with solids and spaces, planes and light, in pictures of apples and tables and walls and trees that nobody wanted? It was, I am sorry to say, the capitalist system, which gave him a private income sufficient for his needs. Now our friend, in his admirable enthusiasm, no doubt imagined that Socialism or Communism would have abolished this small private income, but on the other hand would either have found him generous patrons by the hundred or given him a handsome State allowance. But would it? Where would the patrons have come from, when we know it took years for people to understand what he was up to? And what Central Committee, Art Authority or Painters' Union would be willing to grant a good allowance to this morose eccentric with his repulsive daubs? He would probably be told to make himself useful and to stop thinking he was a painter – to try for a job at the gasworks. And I assure you I am not exaggerating, having no desire to make my present task any harder. No, Cezanne and his kind, the original geniuses who develop slowly and cannot be widely appreciated for years and years, offer us a nettle (which is no bad symbol of them) that we shall have to grasp. They are not the sort of mild men who can work in a bank all week (Gaugin tried that) and then do a nice bit of painting on Saturday afternoon and Sunday. These are not men with a hobby but with a solemn vocation, a blazing mission. Now, bring on your Socialist State, which, we will say, takes from one of them his private income, another of them his one wealthy eccentric patron, and the other the sinecure he was lucky enough to obtain, and where are they?

And how do they live while nobody wants what they are doing?

And if we reply that we don't know and have more important things to bother about, then we may be busy creating a society that has said goodbye to any further great achievements and developments in these arts, that may smother its dreary citizens in a mush of mediocrity, that can produce and cherish everything but the beacon blaze of genius, that is losing the leaven from the bread.

Tricky, isn't it? Obviously we cannot afford, in the new society, to allow people to have private incomes or sinecures right and left in the hope that one of them may turn out to be another Cezanne. But here I would add this, in parenthesis. There are – and certainly will be – a large number of pleasant half-jobs, not demanding too much time and energy but requiring men and women of culture, not too responsible positions in libraries, galleries, museums, opera houses, theatres and the like, that seem to me particularly suitable for certain types of artists – not the big volcanic fellows who would blow the place up in a week – but the milder and more modest kinds, the occasional poets or musicians, the dramatist, novelist, essayist or critic who is more fastidious than fertile, the painter who works best at intervals; and I believe by bearing this in mind, we may neatly solve two little problems at the same kind, filling not unimportant if small positions with the right kind of people, and offering opportunity and security to those minor artists who prefer to have some pleasant regular employment outside their art. But now let us grasp the nettle again. Our Socialist State, with no private incomes, eccentric rich patrons or sinecures, we will say, is here; and here too is young Smith, that gawky, rather sullen young man, who is obviously no fool but whose strange pictures or queer sonatas nobody likes.

What is to become of him?

Case of Young Smith

Do not let us delude ourselves. Good taste and judgment in these matters of fine art will not be miraculously bestowed upon the leaders of collectivist society. When young Smith turns up, producing his rum paintings or his almost sinister sonatas, it is probably 50 to 1 that the Committee, probably consisting of educationalists, officials and a few tired old frauds of artists, will promptly turn young Smith down. No scholarship, no grant, no public subsidy, for this young man, who is doing things that nobody wants, will not take good advice, and appears to be not only obstinate and bad-mannered but also not quite right in his head. 'Go earn your living, young man,' they will say to him, 'and if you must go on painting, then do it in your spare time, and take our course of evening classes to improve yourself. Miss Robinson will give you a copy of the Handbook.' And young Smith, who is, please remember, a genuine original genius, one of those rare creatures who seem to arrive here from some other and fierier planet, will certainly reject this well-meant but idiotic advice, and go storming out, to paint or compose day and night even if it means starvation. For this strange young man will be in the grip of profound forces quite beyond the comprehension of any useful member of a Grants Committee. And he cannot – and indeed it is essential that he must not – be tamed. On the other hand, if he starves, if he is humbugged and bullied by officials and psychiatrists, if he feels himself terribly isolated and at war with the community, his precious gifts, the rarest of all, may be lost to us.

It is no use saying: 'Oh well, we'll see that all these brilliant young artists are helped at first. Even if we don't understand what they're trying to do, we'll still help 'em.' If you take that line, then any chap with a bit of impudence can pop in, claiming to be an original genius, and live without working, supported by public funds. Lazy frauds by the score would turn up, finally discrediting all attempts to subsidise the artist in the early stage of his career. No, there is no easy way out there. Indeed, probably there is no easy way out for any genuine young Smith either. No matter how we plan, he may have to risk some bad years, although of course it is characteristic of the artist of real originality and power that he is always ready to take that risk. He cannot do anything else, cannot compromise, because his work is his life, and unless he is attempting to produce that work he feels that he is not living at all and might as well be dead. Now I think I have faced this problem honestly, and it is one that is generally shirked.

I am entitled now, I feel, to indulge in a little optimism. In the first place, I take the view that when people have more leisure and have increased opportunities to study the arts, an original genius, making considerable demands on his audience's understanding of technique, will have a chance of being appreciated earlier in his career. I think something of this sort is already happening. Because there is a lot of rubbish about and people pack in to try to enjoy all kinds of nonsense, we are apt to imagine that there is now less knowledge and appreciation of the arts than there was – say, 30 or 50 or a hundred years ago. This is quite wrong. The fact is, that there is more of everything about the place – more rubbish perhaps, but also more art too. Take a look some time at the monthly bulletin of the Arts Council, with pages and pages devoted to what is happening in each group of counties, concerts by the hundred, repertory and touring companies all up and down the country, exhibitions of pictures and drawings going off in all directions; and then remember that all this represents new activity; and then add to it all that has been continued from before the war; and then add again all the lectures and courses and classes of all the educational bodies; and I think you will arrive with me at the conclusion that although our people today may not know and appreciate as much art as they ought to do, there are certainly far more of them knowing and appreciating it than ever before in our history.

People with a Flair

Now if you turn a mass of people on to the arts, this is what happens. A large number of them will discover a new source of interest and enjoyment, in a rather mild fashion, making a fairly good average audience or public for the arts. But for a certain, much smaller percentage, some particular art will come as a revelation. This is what they have been looking for all their lives.

You run into such persons – often quite rough chaps, or mousy little women – at exhibitions of pictures, concerts, theatres, or browsing in good bookshops; and often they talk with enthusiasm and discrimination of work that you would have thought much too difficult for them. Education and environment have nothing to do with it, for these are people with an odd natural flair for a certain art or for a certain type of expression in that art. And as you never know where they are going to pop up, this is all the more reason why people in general should have an opportunity to experience good art, however original and difficult it may seem to be. The more people have this chance, the more of these natural under-standers and appreciators we shall discover. Now when we come to our difficult fellow, young Smith, the strange original genius, who is not likely to be accepted by the local Committee, it is these folk with the odd flair who may easily save the situation.

The wealthy patron will have gone, but these other people might collectively take his place in helping the young original artist through the first hard period. They cannot spend thousands, but they can spend a pound or two to back their fancy, can easily subscribe enough between them to keep a few young Smiths going until they are really widely appreciated. Not only that, but these born enthusiasts can begin to get to work on the Committees, persuading, arguing, denouncing and bullying, if necessary, until some notice is taken of young

Smith and his work. And there is nothing fanciful here. The process is already at work, and I wish I was as sure of a good supply of original geniuses as I am of the certainty of this growing encouragement. Remember that a people freed from the old host of gnawing anxieties and desperate worries, and sooner or later, we hope, free too from the pressure exerted upon them by big commerical enterprises to entangle them in trivialities (an aspect of capitalism that is too frequently overlooked), and people living in reasonably civilised conditions, will have far more mental energy to spare than they have had in the past. Their minds, as we are beginning to see already, will look for things on which to fasten, and among the arts they will find some of the most exciting of those things.

The Artist Works from Inside

So far as important new works of art are concerned, however, we shall be told by some pessimists that the citizens of the Socialist State will be, in the mournful phrase of the American comic song, 'all dressed up and nowhere to go'. In other words, we shall be told that real art and the Socialist State will find co-existence impossible. That tidy housewife, Socialism, will not take as a husband that disreputable fellow, who is probably an anarchist at heart, who keeps no regular hours, whose values are strange and disturbing, the creative artist; who, in his turn, will refuse to settle down, fill in all his forms and pay his dues, will find no inspiration in this vast hygienic beehive, and will take to drink and despair. I have said that the State must leave the artist alone with his work after creating reasonable conditions for him. There must be no meetings of politicians and bureaucrats telling painters how to paint and musicians how to compose, and no inter-departmental co-ordinating committees handing out ideas and themes from the various Ministries to novelists and dramatists. ('Your next job, old boy, is a three-act comedy about bottling fruit in the Women's Institutes. Sorry, old boy, but you must – it's a definite directive from the FAO through the COI.') We cannot accept the view that artists are mere stooges for the Public Relations departments. An artist has to be a technician, but he has also to be something more than a technician. And if this is not recognised, then there may be plenty of bottled fruit, but there will not be much art worth having. And if you say that bottled fruit comes first, you may also find that it comes last too: in short, that art, and all the wonder and insight and glory of it, has vanished from your world, which, all properly tidy and cleaned up, is nothing but a mausoleum of the human spirit. Now when I talk like this to some people, they are deeply shocked, as if I were revealing bourgeois prejudices that they imagined I had lost long ago. 'You of all people!' they cry reproachfully. And then I have to point out that if I often prefer to work with political and social themes, it is because I have chosen those particular themes myself and have not had them imposed upon me. They happen to interest and even excite me, so I make use of them; and I wish far more of my colleagues here would make use of them. But of their own free choice, so far as there is any free choice in this matter. At any rate the compulsion must come from inside, where the real work of bringing them to life will have to be done, and not from outside.

A film producer complained to me the other day that his writers were letting him down. He said he had given them several wonderful ideas for stories, which had excited him, but they were not bringing them to life. I told him that if these ideas of his had excited him so much, he ought to have written the stories, and brought them to life himself; and that he should ask his writers to work on ideas that excited them, for a change. And that is the trouble about the artist, you see. He cannot make it exciting for you until he has first made it exciting for himself. And no CSCAS, which the Central Steering Committee for Art Stimulation would soon be called, even though it be staffed by administrative types on a high level, can go down and light fires in the artist's unconscious mind.

Nevertheless, it does not follow then that there will be a complete divorce between the policies and aims of the State, the various political and economic and social adventures of the community, and the outlook and work of the artists. In the present quarrel, which certain decisions recently taken in Russia emphasized, I believe both parties to be in the right – the politician and the sociologist are entitled to say to the artist: 'Come and help us in our great struggle.' On the other hand, the artist is right to say: 'Take your committees away from me, and leave me alone with my work.' They are all at cross-purposes, punching at each other in a thick fog, as the nations themselves are, these days. Leave the artist alone with his work – certainly; and make no attempt, doomed to failure, at dictation. But I believe that if you make the artist feel that once again, after a long exile on the outer rim of society, he is back again in the centre, secure in the real heart of the community, which looks to him for wonder and insight and glory, then artists of all kinds will find themselves naturally tending to bring their own work into line with the broad aims and the various adventures of the community. He will do what the politician or the educator or the sociologist would like him to do, not because he has been told to do it that way, but because he has found his inspiration at the same source. And this would be an excellent thing for many artists, who cannot help feeling obscurely that something is wrong, that the artery is hardened and narrow, that new and refreshing springs should be unsealed for them, that somehow they are cut off from the great common movements of their age.

A great deal of the art of our time, in spite of its superb technical equipment, has suffered because the artist has assumed that a kind of exile from the broad community is his natural lot. Alone with his work, determined to make it as perfect as possible, he feels for the time being that he is in the centre and heart of things; but then as soon as he leaves his work, goes into the street or a pub or looks at the newspaper, he begins to feel a wistful eccentric on the edge of society, a belated Shakespearean fool singing in a high cracked voice in the storm on the heath. Thus many of these artists, men of undoubted genius, have been driven more and more, further and further, into the dark recesses of their own being, from which they have brought us only elaborately detailed reports of their own doubts and torments. This is particularly seen in what should be the popular and universally accepted art of the Novel, in which contemporary men of genius, men like Proust, Joyce, Gide, Mann, are admired by the comparative few for their great gifts and completely unread and misunderstood by the many, who can still read and enjoy Tolstoy and Balzac and Dickens. Time after time we have seen these great gifts, which should have illuminated like suns the lives of millions, narrowed to a faint radiance for a mere handful of aesthetes, just because circumstances have so compelled the writers to turn inward that they have neither realised their own full natures nor done for their art what previous men of genius did for theirs.

I say then, that if the artist discovers himself near the centre again, as one of the community's essential interpreters, art itself will do what no committee or union can compel it to do.

The Flower of Art

Great art probably depends on a balance between the outward view of man in society and the inward view of man exploring the depths of his own psyche. The artist swings, as indeed we must all do, between the extremes of the organised community and the Collective Unconscious, the vast outward world of human society and the dark mysterious ocean of that Unconscious from which inspiration comes. Look too long in one way or the other, and the balance is lost, and the art misses greatness. But there is something else too. Great art seems to arrive for those communities that genuinely and warmly demand it. In 70 years the small single city of Florence produced more great work in the visual arts than the whole continent of America has produced in 200 years. Why? Because the Florentines had a passion for the visual arts and the Americans have not, and once the community has a passion it is as if some queer force were generated just below the surface of its life, exploding in works of genius. If the English were as excited about poetic tragedies and string quartets as they are about Test Matches, then very soon, I am prepared to prophesy, we should bring forth the most enchanting poetic tragedies and string quartets. And indeed, sometimes when I glance at those articles, which know nothing of any paper shortage, bemoaning our recent lack of success in this field of international sport, I wonder if the editors, by still giving so much space and attention to sport and so little to the arts, are not perhaps backing the wrong horse, for it may well be that we English, who led the way in these games for so long, have really now moved away from them in the depths of our collective being; and are now ready for new and more enduring triumphs, are beginning to cry in the darkness for the colour and grace and glory of the arts. I commend the idea, sketchy though it is, to the makers of our Socialist State, who would then find the arts, both as creation and appreciation, leavening the heavy and soggy dough of our society. We might then find it possible to achieve a community in which every citizen felt himself to be something of an artist and every artist knew himself to be a citizen. But the State can only clear the ground and build a wall against the cold wind: it cannot pull out of the dark soil the flower of art; only the artist can do that. I always remember with some feeling a story my wife told me. She stayed once in France at the house of a musician who had been blind since childhood.

This musician told her how he had been given an edition in braille of Beethoven's sonatas, and how, as his fingers had moved over the raised dots, the full wonder and grandeur and beauty of these compositions had burst upon him in his darkness, and he had wept. A deaf musician, hearing in imagination the passion and glory of his themes, makes some marks on paper, and then years and years afterwards these marks are changed to little lumps and scratches so that a blind man's fingers read them and from those fingers a message goes flaming to blaze in the windowless mind, and after a century a stoical man breaks down and cries.

When I remember that story, Man seems great again, and no matter how vast and mysterious this universe, his heart and mind are at home in it. No State can work miracles like these. All it can do is to cherish them.

Postscript to the Fabian Lecture

WHAT THE GOVERNMENT SHOULD
DO FOR THE ARTS HERE AND NOW

In my lecture I pointed out that if the State wants plenty of good art, it must create favourable conditions for the artist; and I went on to say that these conditions did not exist in this country now and that I knew of no plans to bring them into existence in the near future. I added that other governments, far worse off than ours, were already doing more for their arts and artists than our government is doing. I could have gone further than this and declared, with perfect truth, that many artists of different kinds here now find themselves much worse off than ever before and are beginning to wonder if the Labour Party cares a rap whether they live or die. The position is all the more serious because our people need all the lift that the arts can give them.

There is a further danger, now just in sight. If the wrong people control the platforms on which the artist must appear, there is more than a chance that such people will exercise that control for political ends. (This is already beginning to happen in the Theatre, where plays of no great merit that satirise or attack Government policy are given particularly favourable opportunities in the West End. It will be noticed too that British films, which should be using themes that deal with broad social issues in a post-war spirit, are mostly avoiding such themes.) Not being in the confidence of our present ministers, I cannot say why they are not aware of these dangers or why they are doing so little for the arts and the artists, but if they were challenged I imagine that their reply would be something like this: 'Yes, that's all very well. But look at our programme. We have too many other more important things to do. All this stuff can wait. Give us time, and we will offer you a Plan For Leisure.' This is, as I suggested in my lecture, the icing-on-the-cake attitude towards art, and I believe it to be all wrong. We need the arts, and all the great lift of the spirit they can give us, urgently here and now. The dough must have its leaven; and routine pep talks from tired politicians are not, in my view, the right kind of leaven. No doubt I shall be told that most people in this country, in spite of many recent examples to the contrary, do not care tuppence for all your arts; that the total works of Shakespeare, Rembrandt, Beethoven, to say nothing of Shaw, Augustus John, Vaughan Williams, would not raise the faintest cheer at any Trade Union meeting. To which my instant reply would be that, even if this should be true, the arts in one form or another mean a great deal to sensitive, alert and articulate people, and that these are the very people who soon sway all the rest. (Just let them swing away from the Left – and see what happens.)

And that is not all. For more than half a century the various Socialist and Labour parties have been telling us that they, and they alone, care for the artist and realise the importance of art in the life of the community. Thus the pledge was made, and now the time is here when that pledge must be redeemed.

Why Feed Education and Starve the Arts?

The Ministry of Education or the Arts Council should call a conference, representative of all the arts, that could examine the present situation in detail and could then draw up a programme of aid to the arts, in consultation with official advisers.

In my view it is absurd to plan and allot vast sums of money to gigantic educational schemes if the environment of our young people, with all its gigantic uneducating influences, is to be left untouched; and among the chief factors that create a good environment are proper conditions for the arts and the artists. For example, what is the use of spending hundreds of thousands of pounds every year teaching children that Shakespeare is a great dramatist, if every playhouse accessible to those children and their parents is completely controlled by men who are determined to present nothing but leg shows and stupid farces? Why have art teachers if real painters are nearly starving? Why teach music and then offer conductors and symphonic players not a glimpse of security? Why have elaborate courses, at the public expense, on English Literature, and yet allow some of the best contemporary books to be out of print for want of paper and binding?

Why spend millions preparing children to enjoy a cultured leisure, and then, because we say we cannot afford anything else, turn them loose in a world of idiotic films, greyhound tracks, fun fairs, and pornographic trash? And, for that matter, why feed a British Council to spread British culture abroad, and yet go on starving that culture at home? But such questions are too easy to ask, if hard to answer. The conference on Aid to the Arts should be called as soon as possible. Any person attending this conference may find the following notes of some use, but nobody realises better than I do how woefully inadequate they are. My excuse is that they have had to be written against time, and during a holiday season when it has been impossible for me to collect material from all the necessary sources or to have any discussion with various representatives of the arts. But inadequate though they are, they are better than nothing, and may at least provide a few jumping-off places for those who are interested.

Visual Arts

First, more materials and implements for artists. Paints, canvases and brushes are now almost unobtainable. I suggested at the UNESCO Conference in Paris, where it was subsequently adopted as part of the 1947 programme, that UNESCO should conduct an international enquiry into the manufacture and distribution of artists' materials and implements, as some countries are desperately short and other countries still have a fair supply. The British Government should acquaint itself with the result of this enquiry, and should instruct the Board of Trade or the Ministry of Supply to do everything possible to encourage the production or importation of such materials and implements. We have now some excellent schools of painting here; there is a growing interest in the visual arts; so it is high time a determined attempt was made to remedy these shortages.

Next, the grants to galleries should be extended and enlarged. Until this last year the Tate Gallery, which houses the principal collection of British Art, received no grant at all, and even now its grant is much too small. It is all very well taxing and death-dutying large fortunes out of existence, but some of the rich did buy and donate good pictures to public galleries, and the Government that has taken their money might at least fulfil some of their obligations. In the same way, the Artists' General Benevolent Institution, which helps artists in distress, should receive a decent public grant, for under present taxation private persons cannot afford to contribute generously to such funds as these. The Government cannot have it both ways, cannot tax the successful artist ferociously, banish the wealthy patron, and then expect charitable contributions and mutual help to go on as before. On the other hand, I have long felt that by the exercise of a little ingenuity and by some public co-operation, far more could be done for painters. Thus, sellers and buyers of pictures by old masters and the like could be asked to contribute 2½ per cent to a benevolent fund; and the same 2½ per cent could be paid by both seller and buyer every time a picture by a living painter changed hands, the money going to the painter himself, who would then at least make something more out of the pictures he was compelled to sell for small sums early in his career.

Again, as the wealthy patron disappears, the Government, and of course other public bodies, should commission large works of art, otherwise very soon only the artist who keeps to small works will be able to exist. Here again a Government that announces that it is going to change the economic and social life of a nation must face its responsibilities. We commissioned a lot of good work during the war, through the War Artists Commission; and the same machinery could be set in motion for peace time, when there are even better subjects for the artists to be found in various aspects of our communal life.

Art and Buildings

Finally, if the building shortage is to continue, professional artists are entitled to some special consideration, because they cannot work anywhere. If studios are scarce, then artists should be entitled to buy or rent them long before they are let to people who merely want to give parties in a large fancy room. If this means interfering with somebody's liberty, then interfere with it; for after all what may be merely a whim to some studio-hunter may be a matter of life-and-death to a painter. And here let me add – for it applies to the other arts, too – that in this important matter of controlling the use of special buildings, such as studios and concert rooms and, above all, theatres, we are now in an awful muddle and mess, just because the Government has not had the courage to be consistent. While building itself is severely controlled, existing buildings should also be controlled. By forbidding the erection of new buildings, you put an end to free enterprise and competition, and at the same time, if you do not exercise further control, you confer upon present owners a most powerful and unjust monopoly. An artist cannot build a studio, but the owner of ten studios can let them all to stockbrokers with Bohemian wives. A new group of theatre workers cannot build a playhouse in the West End, but the Oxford Group can acquire one. New concert halls cannot be put up, but existing concert halls can be turned into cinemas or dance rooms. Just where Government control should begin in earnest, it stops. It cannot be easy to combine the worst features of capitalism and Socialism, but we seem to have achieved something like this combination at present in this matter of buildings.

Music

First, we are desperately short of good concert halls, especially large ones, for symphony concerts. I doubt if there are six really adequate concert halls in the whole country. (There is not one in Central London, although there are now more concerts in London than in any other city in the world.) Nor can it be said there is no demand for them, for the post-war public is a concert-going public. Houses, hospitals, schools may have to come first, but we must have some good concert halls as soon as possible. It does not follow that the Government should build them, for most of them should be owned by municipalities, but the Government, through the various Ministries concerned, should do everything it can to assist the local authorities. For small mixed concerts, chamber music, string ensembles, the Arts Council is doing excellent work by arranging and subsidising tours. But it will have to do far more for the symphony orchestras, the best of which should be treated as national institutions, as most of the great Continental orchestras are. We have plenty of good orchestral players, but too many of them desert the symphony orchestras to do a multitude of odd jobs that bring them in far more money. This is chiefly because these players, remembering lean years in the past and still feeling insecure, are trying to make hay while the sun shines. It is important that members of our best symphonic orchestras should feel secure and should also be conscious of their own importance and dignity.

They should have a definite pension scheme. Moreover, the orchestras should have more time for rehearsal and should not be compelled to perform in public so frequently. (No symphonic orchestras abroad play so often as ours.) Finally, the British Council should make itself responsible for foreign tours of these orchestras. As things are at present, for example, the London Philharmonic presents foreign orchestras, backed by their respective governments, but when it goes abroad itself it has to stand its own losses.

The Arts Council and the British Council should together assist British composers, especially in their early days, by ensuring that their new works are printed as soon as possible and available for wide distribution. Recordings of these works should be speeded up. The demand for new film music of high quality has recently given the British composer a far better chance of earning a living than he used to have, but elderly musicians of distinction should, if necessary, be given Civil List Pensions that really are adequate pensions and not mere pittances. This, of course, applies to other artists, too. It is high time these Civil List Pensions bore some decent relation to the cost of living. The pensions given a hundred years ago would be worth between £700 and £800 today, but no artist today receives such a pension. In this matter we are worse off than our great-grandfathers were.

Theatre

Here the situation is extremely bad, and immediate action is urgently necessary. The Government, through the Arts Council, spends about £65,000 on the Theatre, and most of this is spent not on raising the artistic level of theatrical production but on subsidising repertory and small touring companies. On the other hand, by way of Entertainment Tax the Government takes millions annually from the Theatre. The theatrical life of the country is disorganised and chaotic, and is now chiefly dominated by small powerful groups of theatre owners, whose monopoly cannot be challenged while new theatres cannot be built. And the tragedy of the situation is that both theatre workers and audiences are eager now for drama of a higher quality, but under present conditions, which remain unchallenged by the Government and even encouraged by it, the British people have no chance whatever of having the kind of Theatre they want. In my view, here is a clear case for Government action.

A National Theatre Authority should be created, first to examine and report on present conditions, with special reference to theatre ownership, and then to take action. This Authority should take over the theatrical duties of the Arts Council, which can deal adequately with the visual arts and music but not with the Theatre. A far larger proportion of the money collected in Entertainment Tax should be handed over to this Authority, if only to feed the goose that lays the golden eggs. Three other national companies, similar to the Old Vic, should be formed, and each of them should have two acting companies, one in London and the other on tour, playing real repertory. Municipalities should be encouraged and if necessary assisted to establish Civic Repertory Theatres. For the smaller towns these should be run on the group system. All playhouses should be regarded as part of the public amenities and not as anybody's private property, and their use should be controlled for the public benefit. At present there is nothing to prevent a religious sect buying up half the theatres in London, and the proprietor of fun fairs and flea circuses buying up the rest. While new theatres cannot be built, it is absurd to talk about free enterprise and supply-and-demand; therefore some form of public control is essential.

The Entertainment Tax could be used to encourage genuine theatrical enterprise and to discourage mere profiteering in long runs, which have no artistic value. Thus the tax could be smaller during the first few months of a play's run, while the costs of production have still to be paid off, and then could be increasingly stiffened as the run lengthened. With this system in operation, and with vastly increased subsidies at first for the National Companies, all productions could be required to pay the Tax, and the present difference between profit and non-profit enterprises, which works badly, could be abolished. The idea of allowing nonprofit companies, producing plays of some quality, to retain the tax was well-meant, but in practice it has not worked well, and in some instances the theatre owners, whom the scheme was not intended to benefit, are the very people who have gained most out of it.

Many of the worst evils of our Theatre – the gambling and muddle and waste of commercial managements, the actor's feeling of insecurity, the playwright's feeling of helplessness, the lack of national organisation – cannot be removed by the Government, but only by the combined action of theatre workers themselves. But some of the biggest obstacles could be removed by the Government, working with municipal authorities. And the creation of a National Theatre Authority, representative of the whole dramatic profession, seems to me the first and most important move that the Government should make.

1947

ON CRITICS

I WAS GENERALLY supposed to be embroiled in a permanent feud with dramatic critics. (Bob Benchley, writing in the *New Yorker* about some play of mine he didn't enjoy, ended his notice: 'Now shoot me, Mr Priestley!') Apart from the fact that I often look and sound like a man ready to quarrel with anybody, I cannot understand why I was thought to dislike the critics so much. I did less wrangling with them in public than many other playwrights. Several of them, notably Ivor Brown, were friends of mine. Agate welcomed me most warmly into the Theatre. I received much kindness and many handsome compliments from dramatic critics. The consistently un-friendly notices appeared in papers that, for one reason or another, disliked me anyhow. One influential critic, dead now, did contrive to annoy me every time I produced a new play. If it was a serious play, he would say it was all very well but disappointing because it lacked 'that rich North Country humour we expect from Mr Priestley'. If it was a comedy, he would say it was amusing enough but disappointing again because it lacked 'the serious treatment of a serious theme we expect from Mr Priestley'. For him and his readers apparently I was always writing the wrong play. And I must admit that whenever I made an experiment I immediately lost all the older critics, who declared at once that it was pretentious and that they remembered something just like it in Berlin in 1923. Time after time I was condemned for writing plays that either had too much social content or were too experimental. Not long ago I heard the most successful of our young manager-directors, on television, declaring that old British dramatists could be ignored because their work had not sufficient social content and was never experimental. Ah well!

Margin Released

But once he had entered the world of Theatre, he was always prepared to fight its corner. He in turn became the critic.

Some dramatists seem to think that playgoing is a civic duty. I am not one of them. The Theatre is not a temple of anything; it is what it always was in this country – a place of entertainment. There ought to be something more than entertainment in a good play; but if, first of all, there is not entertainment, then it is not a good play, no matter how fine its emotions, how profound its ideas.

There is nothing startling about the fact that the serious Theatre should be entertaining, or the fact that a good deal of dramatic entertainment should be fit to belong to the serious Theatre. Intelligent adult persons should demand intelligent adult entertainment.

Without knowing what they are doing, quite a number of our dramatic critics are busy hindering and not helping the serious Theatre. I respect the dramatic critic who writes about a play as if it were a private performance for himself, who never mentions box offices, who sees the thing purely as a work of art and not as a social event and a financial enterprise. Many critics assume that their readers are half-witted. They are careful to warn them off any play that has a glimmer of intelligence about it. The result is that they are no longer on the side of the serious Theatre. Time after time I have gone to see serious plays, against which the ordinary cheerful playgoer has been solemnly warned by these critics, and I have seen the audience sit entranced at the end, then burst into a storm of clapping and cheering. They had had a real evening of drama.

It is a pity that dramatic critics are for ever condemned to visit theatres on first nights and no other nights. If they did their playgoing later, they would come to understand the difference between audiences who had been bamboozled in by showmanship and publicity, only to discover that the two-headed calf was yet again a fake, and audiences who were really and actively playgoing, eager, excited, happy audiences.

An intelligent dramatic critic who has enjoyed a play should write about that play in such a fashion as to encourage his readers to go and enjoy it too. It can be done. Now the serious Theatre is battling against horribly heavy odds, and badly needs some fighting champions. If the critic feels that he cannot join in, well and good. But I would remind him of the old song about the negro preacher who was treed by a bear, and whose fervent prayer ended: 'Oh, Lawd, if yo' can't help me, for goodness sake, don't help dat bear.' Keep right out, or join in, Mr Critic, but do not interfere on the wrong side.

Spectator, 19 April 1935

Eight years later he returned to the fray:

There are signs that our people are at last wanting a genuine Theatre, an adult, vital, exciting drama of our own, and dramatic critics can do much to hinder or help the creation of this Theatre and its drama.

Unless our dramatic criticism changes rapidly and radically, we can only succeed in spite of it. Up to now it has been a grave hindrance. There are of course exceptions. The fact that you may trust some particular critic does not weaken my charges against the general level of criticism, which directly influences the public and the Box Office, and may strongly influence writers, players, managers.

The first fault of most of them is that, like their editors and their proprietors, they think of the Theatre as a minor branch of 'show business'. On this commercial basis, a big musical comedy is naturally more important than any play, a star-studded light comedy is more important than any serious play, and any very earnest, out-of-the-ordinary little production is hardly worth mentioning at all.

The next fault is the reporting of new productions without any kind of reference to the idea of the Theatre as a genuine and enduring institution. There is no suggestion in these notices of anybody – writer, director, player – contributing anything to a continuing body of work. Too many of the critics have never begun to think in terms of an English Theatre.

One final charge. There are one or two dramatic critics here who do not commit these sins, who are excellent men of the Theatre themselves, and who have worked magnificently for it in the past. But now they have one grave weakness, which sadly reduces their value to the contemporary Theatre. They are convinced that no further changes are desirable – or indeed really possible – in dramatic technique. Once rebels, they are now reactionaries. Those of us who wish to try a new trick or two are condemned, almost before the curtain has gone up, as being 'pretentious', 'fantastic', 'woolly' and the rest. Nor is it simply a matter of technique. Themes must change as time moves on, and if the public mind can move with it, then so can the critic. There seem to me to be now thousands of younger playgoers who are far ahead of nearly all the critics.

New Statesman, 25 September 1943

Five years later he defined more precisely what he saw as the critic's function.

There are, broadly speaking, three ways in which critics and editors of theatrical periodicals can help our Theatre. They can welcome and examine sympathetically all attempts to give plays a broader and deeper social and philosophical content. They can welcome and examine sympathetically genuine experiments in writing, production, design, acting.

They can welcome and try to appreciate to the full all attempts to raise the standard of production and acting. Let us call these three – Social Content, Experiment, and Higher Standard.

Some newspapers with enormous circulations regularly publish theatrical notices by men who must be rejected on all three counts. All they ask for is the thin little dramatic mixture as before. They merely want to spend the evening in a pleasant familiar haze. A light comedy that is like all the other light comedies of the last forty years, except that it is not acted as well as it used to be, suits them perfectly.

Another mistake, often made by critics intelligent enough to know better, is to assume that any play that challenges them on the Social Content level must offer them a 'message'. This criticism baffles me. I am quite capable of writing messages, being a dogmatic sort of fellow, but it would never occur to me to wrap up a message in a hundred pages of play script. The business of a play is to offer audiences a unique kind of experience, which may stimulate their emotions in a certain fashion. But a message? Incidentally is it only living dramatists who are asked for their messages? What is the message of *Hamlet* or *The Cherry Orchard*?

A few of the older critics, not unappreciative of both Social Content and Higher Standard, always fall down on Experiment, which annoys them. They forget that the naturalistic play that they admire was itself once an experiment, the challenge of an advanced Theatre.

On the Social Content and Experiment counts, the new critics in theatrical periodicals are much sounder that their colleagues elsewhere. They want to see plays that are not afraid of the world we live in, that place before their audiences the great issues of our time. They welcome Experiment and do not sneer at it. But I often find them dangerously unsound in the third department, that of the Higher Standard. They will sometimes praise careless productions and sloppy acting, and do not insist with sufficient rigour on a high standard of performance.

But we must have a higher standard, and the new critics must join us in insisting upon this higher standard. The basis of good Theatre, whatever it may attempt to do, is a magnificent and tireless professional efficiency. There is no magic here, except where occasional flashes of creative imagination play their part. The necessary ingredients are time and trouble and hard work. Incomparably the best productions I have ever seen are those of the Moscow Arts Theatre. Why? Because this company is able to take time and trouble and work hard. Their actors are not by nature any better than ours. Indeed, it is my experience that our actors, difficult as their conditions often are, are the first to welcome any attempt to break away from sloppy improvisation and to substitute for it some hard, close team-work.

It is, I feel, up to the critics now. They should insist on at least a competent standard of production and acting, on all the tools for the job being sharp and clean.

Theatre Newsletter, December 1948

THEATRE OUTLOOK

IN 1946 my father fired off what he called a 'dispatch from the battlefield', assessing frankly the state of Theatre, its value and predicament, at the time, and putting forth suggestions, both passionate and practical, for its survival and development. Some sections referred specifically to factors prevalent at the time, while others have maintained their prescience today. I have selected extracts accordingly.

Introduction

It is necessary to add some comments [to what follows], as certain things have happened in the Theatre [since it was written].

First, the immediate post-war boom in the Theatre has given place, both in the West End and the provinces, to a slump. I doubt if theatres throughout the country are taking more than 50 per cent of what they were taking a year ago. Secondly, there has been some discussion (but not enough) of our theatrical conditions in the House of Commons, where Mr Dalton vaguely promised a possible Working Party to examine these conditions.

Thirdly, representatives of various groups of theatre workers and of various theatrical interests have been meeting to organise a large National Conference of the Theatre, which is due to take place in London in November. It is to be hoped that this Conference will agree that certain reforms are urgently necessary, and will press for immediate action.

The present economics of the Theatre are ruinous and insane. At a time when our audiences are developing a taste for good drama, and clearly need all the inspiration or solace that good drama can give them, there is nobody seriously engaged in theatrical production who is not beginning to feel baffled, frustrated, helpless. (The fact that a few 'smash hits' still more than pay their way does not affect the argument. Aiming at a rapidly dwindling bull's-eye should not be the primary task of the serious theatrical producer.) If, like the Russians, we had large theatres filled to capacity at every performance, perhaps we could pay our way at present theatre prices. But many of our theatres, especially in the West End, are quite small, and throughout the country our patrons like to stay away on Monday (even if they have to stand or be turned away on Saturday night), and will allow sunshine, fog or sleet, or some national crisis to cancel their Theatre-going. Again, although, as I have pointed out in my text, theatre seats are comparatively cheap, not having kept pace with other prices, the public is unwilling to pay more at our box offices and already grumbles at the present rates. Yet it is impossible, on this scale of patronage and at these prices, for us to arrive at a proper relation between our costs and our receipts.

We are gambling with the dice loaded against us. And we should not be gambling at all. Our job – and a full-time hard task it is – is to produce good drama, and not to try working economic miracles.

Some of my colleagues advocate the abolition of the Entertainment Duty on all performances by live players. Others oppose this and prefer to see more non-profit companies brought into existence to operate free from the tax. (This is all right for inexpensive straight plays, but I cannot see a non-profit company raising the initial capital to finance big expensive productions.) Others again, and I am one of them, would like to see a graded Entertainment Duty, with the Treasury returning to the Theatre, by way of subsidies through a National Theatre Authority or the Arts Council, a fair proportion of the money taken out of the Theatre. But even then, there is still the question of control to be settled. In my view, the Theatre at present is not controlled by dramatists, actors, producers or managers, but chiefly by theatre owners, men of property who may or may not have a taste for the drama. The owners not only take too much out of the Theatre, but they also decide what kind of plays shall be produced there.

As I have shown later, it is not that the owners are purely 'commercial', but that they cannot help satisfying their own particular tastes. (And in their place, we should all do the same.) This is not a personal attack upon owners. What I condemn is the property system that allows public amenities and a communal art to be controlled by persons who happen to be rich enough to acquire playhouses. And although there are many other problems, here is the root problem: Who shall own – and therefore control – the playhouses? And everything that has happened since I completed this book has only confirmed me in this opinion.

September 1947

Character and Scope

This book will be personal in tone. There are various good reasons why it should be personal. The Theatre is a subject that demands a more personal approach than do most topics now under discussion. Again, it is fairer to the reader if I make it clear throughout that I am setting down my own opinion and seeing things from my own point of view. Finally the frankly personal tone saves time and fuss and avoids the woolly, pompous manner, all too common among sociologists. And now having planted myself in the scene, I must say something about my qualifications.

Who am I to write a book about the Theatre? The answer that I have had 25 plays produced, many of them in at least a dozen different countries, is not good enough. It is possible for a man to write successful plays and yet not be qualified to write a book about the Theatre. (This is particularly true of English dramatists.) But though I cannot pretend to have spent my life in the Theatre – and any man who has is probably not qualified to write about anything, not even the Theatre – I can reasonably claim to have had a good deal of theatrical experience, apart from the writing and the rehearsing of plays. I have helped to run production companies, both for my own and other people's plays, have had a share in various kinds of theatrical enterprise, have done a bit of everything from financial speculation in the West End to the judging of village amateurs, have visited most of the best playhouses in the world, and have discussed theatrical problems all the way from the Moscow Arts Theatre to the Coketown Twice-Nightly Rep. My experience may not have been remarkably long – about 15 years – but it can be said to have been unusually thick, and sometimes indeed, I have felt, a bit too thick. And so much for my qualifications.

Now for this book. It must take its place among works considering the problems of our democracy. Therefore, it seems to me, it must be neither 'show business' nor yet vaguely 'arty'. It must assume that there is such a thing as the art of Drama, and that this communal art is of considerable value to our new democratic society. It must set the Theatre squarely within the framework of our community, and must then examine its present situation, more especially its economic position (which is often so conveniently ignored), and must go on to consider its future. The questions it must answer are: *What is happening to our Theatre now?*, and then: *What ought to happen to it in the near future?* And let me add that there never was a time in our theatrical history when it was more important to ask and to try to answer these two questions. For we are now in a most curious position.

We might say that the great battle between the friends and enemies of the Theatre is now roaring all round us. We are at once worse off and better off than ever before. We are worse off because the economic conditions of theatrical production are appalling, and all the old faults of the English Theatre are strongly in evidence. We are better off because we have created new audiences with a sharp appetite for good drama, and directors, players, and designers are crying out for serious work, and young playwrights by the dozen are dipping or chewing their pens. It is, some of us feel, Now or Never for the English Theatre. It is touch-and-go whether we resist the final assault of the Old Guard and then go forward to victory, achieving at last a properly organised Theatre, or waver and break, retreating to the miserable commercial muddle we have known before. Finally, we have a Labour Government that is, in theory at least, favourable to these communal arts and has won its way to power by denouncing those economic and social forces that are the enemies of the true Theatre. Perhaps the members of this Government, who have so much else to do, do not understand what is happening, have no notion that the battle is on. I hope this is true – for I should hate to think that they know what is happening and simply do not care – and this is yet one more reason why a book of this kind on the Theatre should be published. And if it reads like a hasty dispatch from the battlefield, then so much the better.

Are We a Dramatic People?

There are some persons here, often persons of influence too, who tell us that we need not bother our heads about the Theatre, which can be left to gesticulating and excitable foreigners, because although we occasionally like to see 'a jolly good show', we are not a people who could ever succeed in the art of Drama. Thus, if you explain to such persons how good the Russian Theatre is, they reply at once that of course all Russians are born for the Theatre, whereas we British are not really good at that sort of thing. (There is, of course, always a strong suggestion here that God created us for worthier tasks.) And it is useless to reply that the native histrionic gifts of the Russians are no better than ours, and that what gives the present Soviet Theatre its immense superiority is its national organisation, based on the recognition of the place of the Theatre in the community. These Podsnaps, equally terrified of generous emotion and new ideas, walk away, shaking their heads. But what are the facts? Obviously a people with no native gifts for or inclination towards drama would be unable to produce many outstanding writers for the Theatre and players of talent. But between Shakespeare, acknowledged the world's greatest dramatist, and Shaw, the foremost living dramatist, we have produced a long glittering galaxy of famous writers for the Theatre, and, to support them, at all periods, actors and actresses of splendid talent. What nation can produce better theatrical records? The Spaniards, the French, the Italians, the Germans, and the Russians have had their great periods; and we have had our blank periods, notably in the 17th century when the Puritans closed all theatres, and during the mid-19th-century years, when both writing and acting were mediocre; but it is doubtful if any nation can produce more outstanding dramatists and players than we can. Moreover, our Theatre from Shakespeare's day onwards, except during a few short periods, has always been a popular Theatre, supported whenever possible by the people themselves. (It is worth remembering that the Elizabethan Theatre owes its chief triumphs to the victory of the popular dramatists over the University wits and admirers of Seneca.) We may have suffered somewhat from the lack of carefully cherished and subsidised court and official theatres, but that has not been the fault of the people themselves, who have always loved the play. The fact is, this notion that the English are undramatic does not apply to the people in general or to the truly national character and genius, but only to a small ruling and official class, created during these last 150 years or so. Everything I know about my fellow-countrymen, below the level of this highly conditioned class, confirms my view that the English, although not given to emotional display, are in fact ruled by a highly dramatic imagination, to which all our leading statesmen instinctively appeal. (Churchill in 1940 understood this.) It is this imagination in the people that so richly appreciates a fruity public character. It is this imagination that insists upon placing certain national defeats, which have a romantic and poetical character, far above many national victories. It is this imagination that has a tenderness for heroic failures. Jung has suggested that the soul of a conquered people enters and dominates the unconscious minds of their conquerors, and the English unconscious is haunted by the soul of the Celt. That is why this island, ostensibly crowded with shopkeepers and mechanics, is so full of lyric poets and ghosts and strange sects and rumours of faerie gold. And that is why the people, so untheatrical in their outward habits, have always turned instinctively to the Theatre, to brood with Hamlet (easily the most popular play of the last two and a half centuries) and gape and roar at the clowns. Playgoing with us is at a deeper and more instinctive level of behaviour than it is with most peoples. It is not official and routine, but dream calling to dream. Not only are we not an undramatic people, but in some respects we are the most dramatic people left on earth. In Shakespeare's time we sent plays and players all over Europe. We are still sending them.

The Enemies of the Theatre

I could venture to say, above, that in some respects we are the most dramatic people left on earth, because I realise only too well how many obstacles our Theatre is compelled to face. Only a people with a deep instinctive feeling for dramatic art would be inclined to challenge such obstacles. As individuals we may have this need for drama, but our society is not Theatre-minded.

The Theatre has kept its place in the hearts of the people, but not in the Community. Compare our official treatment of the dramatic with that of the visual arts. The State and our cities build and maintain museums and art galleries, spend public money acquiring pictures and pieces of sculpture, and organise solemn official openings of annual exhibitions. Every town of any size has its Art School. But the Theatre, which is far closer to our people than the visual arts, does not receive such patronage. It is regarded as a commercial affair, part of the entertainment business, and playgoing, like smoking and drinking wine and spirits, is severely taxed. Now most of these museums and art galleries and schools were established during the 19th century, and this fact, I believe, gives us a valuable clue to the different treatment of the dramatic and visual arts. The two dominating classes in the 19th century were the landed gentry and the new-rich manu-facturing class of the Midlands and the North. The latter did not care about the Theatre, often because they had puritanical prejudices against it. (In my youth, in Bradford, I knew a lot of families that never visited the Theatre, only 40 years ago.) The landed gentry liked a country-house life and sport, and generally thought of the stage as a show of pretty women, an attitude of mind that still persists in the West End. A society dominated by these two types of mind would not be likely to give the Theatre much official patronage. It would never occur to such persons that London ought to have theatres as far removed from commercial speculation as the British Museum is. There might be occasional royal visits or command perform-ances at Windsor; an Irving might be given a knighthood; but there would be a strong feeling in the House of Commons, which always had its share of Puritans, that the State could hardly be expected to recognise the existence of the Theatre, with all its commercial high jinks. Moreover, English poli-ticians, taking part in the non-stop drama of Westminster, have usually neither the time nor the inclination to do much serious playgoing. It is doubtful if even now many Labour members realise how shamefully this communal art, for which we have a native genius, has been neglected, abused and prostituted, and how much we are missing by not giving it its rightful place in our society.

As a dramatist I hardly ever visit a continental capital without feeling at once more at home there, just as a man of the Theatre, than I am in London. I hardly ever visit a continental theatre that is producing one of my plays without feeling a welcome change in the atmosphere. These people see the Theatre as I do, and treat the drama as a serious and important communal activity. (Once again I repeat that they have no more natural aptitude for it than we have.) They take for granted what we have to fight for here. It is not because their ordinary folk are friendlier to the Theatre than ours are, but because the enemies of the drama are absent and their society is more Theatre-minded.

Among those enemies, here must be reckoned now a very large section of our Press, both London and provincial, which gives the minimum space and serious attention to the drama and makes no pretence of having any real theatrical values, lumping legs and Lear in one messy hotch-potch of 'show business'. At least two thirds of our attempts at dramatic criticism are no longer even honest reporting, show no signs of taste, sensitiveness, or technical knowledge, and are well below the level of the average member of the audience. Some newspapers are clearly bent on challenging the very existence of the serious Theatre, not only do not help but deliberately hinder the work of local enthusiasts, and obviously hope that their readers will prefer to accept whatever Hollywood chooses to send them. Then, among other enemies of the Theatre, must be reckoned those types who see in theatrical management and speculation an enticing Monte Carlo atmosphere of easy money, pretty women, and bright lights. I do not myself object to the so-called 'commercial manager' as such, although, as we shall see, I believe that a large section of the Theatre should be taken out of the control of commercial managements. I do not accept the view that because a man expects to make a profit out of his theatrical ventures he is necessarily an enemy of my kind of Theatre. I have worked with managers of this kind, men of taste and integrity, who have done good service to the Theatre, and I see no reason why a select few of them should not continue to serve it well. My objection to most commercial managers is not that they want a reasonable return on their capital, but that they insist upon moulding the Theatre to their own dreary taste and outlook. The fact is, a man cannot produce plays as if he were merely manufacturing hairpins. This is a very personal business. And he who pays the piper likes to call the tune; indeed, after a time he insists upon it, and piper-payers are apt to enjoy very poor tunes. A man with a vulgar mind will insist upon offering the public stupid and vulgar productions, and in doing so he may claim the services of players who could be doing good work elsewhere, and may occupy play-houses that are in urgent demand. And it should be remembered that public taste is not something fixed and unalterable; it can be manipulated, raised, and depressed to some extent; and if people want to go to the Theatre, a man who has favourite players under contract and is able to buy or rent good playhouses will be able for some time to indulge his own bad taste while making rather than losing his money. Wartime, with its increased demand for any kind of entertainment and its lowering of standards, always brings up a nasty crop of these managers, whose names, generally splashed all over their productions, are rarely connected with anything good and original. Most of them take little or no trouble to discover promising new work, are delighted to import second-rate Broadway farces, and frequently fall back on revivals of no particular merit. Managers of this kind, who like easy flashy successes and resent the formidable demands made by the art of drama, would be better employed in variety and cabaret entertainment, from which most of them came, and tend merely to be a nuisance in the legitimate field.

[...]

Playgoers as Enemies

Large numbers of playgoers, both in London and the provinces, must be classed as enemies of good Theatre. I have already mentioned the half-witted mobs in provincial cities who visit theatres only to see film stars in the flesh. The presence of one or two film names in a cast can add a thousand pounds a week to the returns in some of the larger theatres. And this nonsense is having a very bad influence on casting. If a play is to be toured before opening in London, then an indifferent young actress with a film reputation would probably be given a leading part in preference to a really excellent actress who does not happen to have worked in films. But then the public must be blamed for the star system. It is they who insist upon flocking to see certain individual performers. There are, or course, some plays that demand one or two star players of exceptional skill, charm, and magnetism, who can, if neces-sary, be surrounded by a number of droning stooges, in productions that look like nothing on earth.

But at least 80 per cent of the best modern plays ask for fine teamwork, rather than stars and stooges, and a Theatre whose playgoers insist upon stars instead of well-trained and experienced groups of players will not be properly equipped to produce such plays. Elderly romantic critics, remembering the golden nights of their youth, may tell us that all this talk of teamwork is bosh and that the Theatre is merely the setting for a few huge extravagant personalities; but we shall do well not to listen to these nostalgic fabulists, and to remember that from Chekhov onwards the best modern dramatists, who are more important than the critics, have clearly been of the opposite opinion. The public, then, needs to be educated to appreciate and to be loyal to the team, the company, and to remove its patronage from the star system, which would then soon collapse. And the result would be a much greater demand for better writing, better producing, and better acting all round. The gain would be immense.

Then there are thousands of innocent playgoers, especially those who visit London once or twice a year to do their playgoing, who would benefit immeasurably, who would have at last a chance to see what good Theatre is, if they were no longer hoodwinked by the 'long run' standard. It is high time people were told the truth about this, and I have never understood why editors of theatrical year-books and the like, men who must know better, help to keep up the illusion. Now it is true that a play may have a long run simply because from the first it is a smashing success. But many plays have had long runs for other reasons. Suppose, for example, a play happens to have only one set, only four or five characters, and opens in a theatre that is not expensive to run. It is not a great success; it is not a failure; and for some time it just 'ticks over', neither making much money nor losing much. Such a play can be kept going for a year or so – and if its weekly costs are small it may have been able to weather some very bad periods – then after that it begins to acquire a prestige and a momentum as a long-run play. Not through merit but longevity it will achieve a reputation and be talked about, especially in places far from London, until at last it becomes one of the productions that every visitor must try to see, and then the box-office manager (who perhaps gave it a life of three weeks after the first night) finds himself selling out the house night after night, week after week, month after month.

And the visitors pack in to see a mechanical performance, long stereotyped, of a second-rate little piece, and then wonder why they are disappointed. Too often they have been humbugged by the vanity of playwrights, the greed of managers, and their own ignorance and lack of interest in theatrical affairs. This whole 'long run' nonsense ought to be dropped. It is bad for playwrights, players, and the public. No production is worth seeing after it has been running, without a break, for a year. At a time when theatres are in urgent demand, I should like to see the Entertainment Tax so adjusted that in the first months, when they still have their initial costs to pay off, productions are taxed lightly, paying a mere token; but as the run goes on and on, with everybody determined to squeeze the orange dry, the tax should rise steeply, thus encouraging artistic enterprise and a reasonable turnover of productions for the benefit of the London playgoer (after all, his theatres are part of his amenities), and sharply discouraging this lingering squeezing-out of profits. And if we had a popular press that was in favour of good Theatre, instead of a messy hotch-potch of 'show business', it could do a great deal to disillusion its readers about these long runs and to persuade them, for their own benefit, to adopt truer standards of judgement.

[...]

Setting the Stage

We must stop seeing the Theatre as a hazy muddle of 'show business', a vague lucky dip, out of which a few fascinating and glamorous personalities are fortunate enough to pluck glittering 'successes'. Let us sweep away all this gossip column rubbish. Leave 'show business' to Broadway and Hollywood. Never mind about the fascinating and glamorous personalities. Stop bothering about glittering successes. Switch off the coloured spotlights, and let the gamblers stay with their green turf and tables. We ought to think of the Theatre as it looks during an early rehearsal on a winter morning, cold and rather dirty, with the players in old clothes looking pinched and dreary, with no lights, no orchestra, no applause, no glamour and excitement. But if the play, director, and players are all of the right sort, something wonderful is beginning to happen, something is taking shape, there is a creative action in progress, a delicate, intensely personal and yet corporate affair; and one night the people will come crowding in, the curtain will go up – and there will be magic. And it is this Theatre, this scene of individual perceptions and co-operative effort, this workshop of dramatic ideas and emotions, that we must keep in mind. The work is hard, if it is to be done properly, and needs everybody's full attention. There should be complete freedom from all feeling of insecurity, all worry about pay packets and last month's bills. The actors should not feel they are mere counters in somebody's gambling game. Nor should they feel that, here in their playhouse, they are making an isolated effort, are engaged in something odd and eccentric, are playing the fool in a corner. They should know that their playhouse has its own place in the whole wide scheme of the British Theatre, that there are stout ladders to higher levels of their art, that they themselves are good and valuable citizens, that the Theatre is not something existing precariously on the edge of the community, but is set squarely inside it, in an honoured position. Knowing all this, then they can get on with their work properly. And that work, I maintain, should not be attempted in an over-charged, super-heated and unhealthy atmosphere of great glittering successes and terrible ghastly failures. Too much, in my opinion, is made of both these; the ups and downs are monstrously magnified; our present Theatre has too many hangers-on shouting the odds. What we need is an atmosphere of high professional skill, earnest co-operation, loyal teamwork lit with unfading gleams of the genuine artist's enthusiasm. We need, too, a Theatre that attracts to itself plenty of virile men and deeply feminine women, and is something better than an exhibition of sexual oddities and perversions. We need, in fact, more psychological maleness and femaleness, and a good deal less sexiness. We want a Theatre that is not a mere shopwindow for pretty young women on the make and posturing introverts. In this Theatre the stage and not the stage door will be all-important. It will be a place where serious professional men and women, properly trained and well equipped, go to work, as surgeons and physicians go to work in a hospital. Let us clear away all the silly nonsense, the muddle, the gambling, the insecurity, the exhibitionism, the cheap inflated egos, and start with a clean bare stage, solidly set in the community and linked with hundreds of similar sensible organisations, a stage on which something good and true and glowing can be created. And I swear that if we will only adopt this new viewpoint, put the Theatre where it belongs, organise it nationally, then the results, within the space of even a few years, will be astonishing. Knowing only too well what a chaos our theatrical life has been, and how great the obstacles have proved themselves to be, I have long marvelled at what we have been able to accomplish on our stages. Bring order into this chaos, remove the obstacles, and I believe we could astonish the world.

The Apex of the Pyramid

We should see our national Theatre organization as a kind of pyramid, with every level of skill, experience, and accomplishment joined to the level above and below it, with steps leading from the base to the apex. On each level there will be the sort of friendly rivalry that gives an additional zest to the job, but between the levels there will be co-operation rather than competition. As in the Soviet Union now – and it is this that gives the Soviet Theatre its strength – the artists on the high levels will help those below, and just as young directors, players, designers of exceptional talent will move up, so too experienced theatre workers will deliberately move down, to give a lift to the less experienced. At the apex of this pyramid, as a shining example and inspiration to the whole Theatre of the nation, there should be several companies of the highest possible excellence, companies that are as far removed from the atmosphere of commercial gambling, profit and loss, cheapjack show business, hasty improvisation, as the National Gallery is. Each of these companies should be a public corporation, financed in the first place, and afterwards guaranteed against loss, by the State. (I doubt if they would lose very much after the first few years, and the money to finance them would come from the Entertainment Duty revenue, and would, of course, represent a very small proportion of what is annually taken out of the Theatre by the Treasury.) Obviously, one of these companies would be the Old Vic, but it would be necessary, in my opinion, to create at least two, probably three, more, all of them on the same level as National Theatre companies. They would not all try to do the same kind of production. Two of them might tend to concentrate on Shakespeare and larger costume productions, while the other two might be at once more modern and more experimental.

(I am trying to work out a rough pattern here, and wish to avoid any discussion of individual merit, but to show what I have in mind, I suggest that John Gielgud's recent Haymarket Company could have served as the nucleus of the second classical-and-costume company, as companion to the Old Vic; and directors with the experience and ability of, say, Basil Dean, Tyrone Guthrie, Michael MacOwan, could be invited to organise and run, with the help of other directors, the two more modern and experimental companies.) On the lines of the chief continental theatres and on those the Old Vic is working along now, each of these national companies would be a complete self-contained theatrical unit, with its own school, studios, and workshops, and, of course, its own headquarters theatre in London. But each company, while playing most of the year in London, would be large enough to have at least one group of productions either touring the provinces or abroad. And they would all be genuine repertory companies, as the Old Vic – to its everlasting credit – is already. This means that if there were four of these national companies, and each of them followed the present example of the Old Vic, then any visitor to London would in any one week during the full season have the choice of no less than twelve first-class productions, while twelve equally good productions would be on tour. The companies would be responsible to a National Theatre Authority, which would demand from them a very high standard of work, but would also at the same time make sure that they were given the highest possible priority for everything they required. Players in these companies would be reasonably well paid, although not on the highest commercial rates, could have short- or long-term contracts, and might be given leave of absence, sometimes to act in films, sometimes to direct or help civic or similar companies. But once these national companies were firmly established, they might do well to follow the excellent example of the Moscow Arts Theatre, and keep their actors much longer at rehearsal, but actually playing less frequently than the Old Vic does at present. Finally, several years' continuous service in any of these companies should entitle a director, player, designer, or technician to some honour that would carry with it certain privileges.

These national companies would do far more than offer our audiences a certain number of first-class productions, all created in the right atmosphere. They would give an immense lift to the whole Theatre. The only people they would discourage would be the speculators, parasites, shoddy impresarios. Everybody else connected with the Theatre would feel a lightening of the spirit. Men and women working in little theatres in remote small towns would work better because they knew about these national companies. It is not merely that such companies could set high standards and serve as shining examples, although this service could hardly be overestimated. But merely to know that these great companies existed, and were able to do their work free at last from all the old dark obstacles, all the miserable doubts and difficulties, devoting all their time and energy to the problems of their art, would itself be a grand inspiration. (I know myself how much I owe to the visits I paid to the Moscow Arts Theatre and to the talks I had there; and, after all, Moscow is far away.) Already the splendid success of the Old Vic during these last two years or so has brought hope and a new confidence to our younger actors and actresses, who no longer feel that our whole theatrical world is a treacherous jungle. Imagine what four such companies, existing on a clear sunlit summit high above this jungle, could do. The very youngest student, on his or her first day at the dramatic school, would feel at once more hopeful and more determined. Let us, then, make certain of this apex to the whole pyramid of our national drama.

Civic Theatres

All our cities and larger towns should have at least two goodsized playhouses. One of them would be occupied by touring companies, including those of the three or four National Companies, which would bring a small repertory of productions and would probably remain several weeks. [...] The other playhouse in these cities and larger towns should be that of the Civic Theatre. These companies should be like the national companies, but, of course, on a more modest scale. They should, wherever possible, be run neither by the municipal authorities nor private groups, but by public corporations, jointly financed by the municipality, the Arts Council, and private contributions. They should be genuine and, if possible, self-contained repertory theatres, and in the more important cities the companies should be large enough to send out locally small touring groups, composed chiefly of junior players. These Civic Theatres should be regarded as being just as much an essential part of the amenities of the place as the libraries, art galleries, and parks. Cities like Liverpool, Manchester, Birmingham, should have Civic Theatres of considerable size and importance, and local patriotism and pride should be roused in their service. Where the regional feeling is strong, as it is in the North (and, of course, in Scotland), the younger dramatists in the neighbourhood should be encouraged to qualify for an entrance into the repertory. On the other hand, plays written in the first place to please rather smart silly people in the West End should no longer be given any preference. These Civic Theatres should develop styles of their own, styles that would reflect something of the local character and outlook. Thus, Manchester's Civic Theatre would be determinedly, and even grimly, Mancunian. Many of the plays might be chosen from the world's best dramatic literature, but the presentation of them on these particular stages could suggest the character of their several regions. I shall probably be told by drama enthusiasts in many of these cities that they and their friends have already tried to establish theatres more or less of this kind and that most of these attempts, after desperate struggles, have failed. But although conditions are far more favourable now than they were when these attempts were made, before the war, because the potential audiences for good Theatre are much larger and there is far more money about, I think the Civic Theatre idea could still be a failure if the effort to realise it were to be made by small private groups, working independently and without much capital. These Civic Theatres should be part of a national scheme, backed by the Ministry of Education, through the Arts Council, local educational authorities, and various professional and cultural organisations. Each of them should be a public and not a private enterprise, a truly civic affair. It must not be a matter of spending a few hundred pounds trying to run a dingy little mission hall as a theatre, with the cheapest possible actors, and production costs cut to the bone. Our cities do not try to run art galleries by taking a disused garage and putting a few bargain daubs into it. On that dismal level hardly anything can succeed. That is not the way to do these things. These Civic Theatres must be generously supplied with initial capital, carefully but not meanly planned, firmly rooted in municipal life, and inaugurated with a flourish and a bang. On these lines they can succeed, even financially, although there may be a fairly substantial debt hanging over them during the first few years. Their greatest problem will be handed to them by our old enemy, Bricks and Mortar. These Civic Theatres should own their own playhouses, specially built to house a good repertory company (and many of our existing theatres lack the necessary accommodation backstage) and to provide seats not for an audience of three or four hundred, but for 1200 to 1500 persons. (The Little Theatre is all very well, particu-larly as a gesture of defiance to the big commercial chap, but the Civic Theatres of large cities cannot possibly be tiny playhouses. This is to begin by admitting defeat.) Meanwhile, most of these cities have at least two good-sized theatres, of which one will serve to house the Civic company. No doubt the owner of such a theatre has his own ideas, which he is not likely to change just because he is approached by a small group of drama enthusiasts. But a properly financed public corporation, with some civic authority behind it, is a very different matter, especially if its plans have been given wide publicity. As things are, there is still nothing to prevent a theatre-owner from defying the whole town, but such an owner would be well advised to accept a reasonable rent and the heightened prestige of his playhouse as against a feud with the municipal authorities and half his patrons. So far as our bricks-and-mortar men believe in anything, they believe in show business; and show business is notoriously sensitive to publicity. Thus, even this problem, given the right organisation to tackle it, is by no means beyond an early solution.

One last point. It may be asked why a Civic Theatre should be run by a public corporation, created for the purpose, and not by the municipal authority itself. There are two reasons for this. First, it is far easier for a public corporation to accept grants from various sources; and many municipal authorities have at present no powers under which they are entitled to spend money on a theatre. Again, the Government, through the Arts Council or some similar department, may be unable to contribute funds to a municipal enterprise. And, obviously, it is better to arrange matters so that the Civic Theatre can be financed in as many different ways as possible. This, then, is the financial reason. The other may be said to be a political one. If the municipality directly controls the Civic Theatre, its appointments, especially the important one of Director, may be considered to be political, coloured with the red or blue tints of the party in power. It would be a pity if a Civic Theatre had to have a different Director after a shift in parties in the City Council. Nor can I agree – as many people would no doubt argue – that we do not think along such lines in this country. I have no ambitions myself in this direction; nevertheless, I do not think I would make a bad Director of a Civic Theatre – but how many Tory Town Councils would let me continue in the job? Unlike gas and sewage and the

upkeep of parks, the Theatre is apt to arouse political prejudices; and so the safer form of organisation is the public
corporation, with some specimens of City Fathers on the
board. But, of course, they must not arrive empty-handed.

The Amateur Theatre

The Amateur Theatre is a whole world in itself. When one
quits the high level of serious, hard-working groups such as
the Newport Little Theatre, the Questors of Ealing, the
Highbury Little Theatre at Sutton Coldfield, to mention only
a few out of scores, we descend through the cheerful limbo of
hockey-club Thespians and factory Strollers, and then reach
a wide vague region in which play-producing and acting are
educational activities, and the pleasure of the audience comes
a poor second to the recreation and training of the players.
All that needs to be said here about all this work and play in
schools, youth clubs, and the like, is that it will gain
immensely through most of the proposals already made in
this section. Furthermore, it seems to me absurd to spend
time and money organising play production as a part of
education, whether juvenile or adult, in a country that makes
no attempt to organise its professional Theatre properly. If it
were left to me I would not spend a penny more on these
educational-dramatic activities until I had made certain that
our best dramatists had good theatres and companies ready
for their work. If we do not propose to put our whole theatrical
house in order, then we might as well stop lecturing about
and teaching the drama. What is the use of advertising for
still more drama leaders of youth clubs and the rest if our
best writers and producers and players are in despair because
the Theatre itself is such a hopeless muddle and mess?

But both the good professionals and the serious amateurs
should try a little co-operation to pull the Theatre, that is,
the whole dramatic life of the country, out of the mess. Let

us admit that the best groups of amateurs now go to work on a higher level than that of many professionals, who have a living to earn and often the most desperate conditions to face. That is no reason why Little Theatre groups should often regard their work as an end in itself, should refuse to support their nearest repertory neighbour, should announce they are always too busy reading and rehearsing and discussing to do any serious playgoing, and should even demand that efforts to establish a creative Theatre organisation nationally should be diverted to building up the amateur movement. They overlook the all-important fact that if there had not been some professional theatre workers *somewhere*, they would never have known what to do or how to do it. And when I have met a successful serious amateur group that has evolved its plays, its ideas of production and acting, out of its own inner consciousness, then I will publicly retract the above statement. Meanwhile, it will be a serious matter for the new Theatre if the opposition to professional Civic Theatres should come from the local amateurs, who wish to claim the only suitable building for themselves. There may have to be some sharing, of course, as there already is in some places; and out of this sharing, let us hope, some genuine co-operation may emerge, although preferably not in the mixing of professional and amateur companies. The relationship can be close, but the work should be separate. The professionals, however, can assist with direction, the designing and building of sets, costumes, lighting, and both parties can make use of dramatic schools, like those at Bristol and Bradford, that offer evening as well as full-time day classes.

Then in all but the larger cities, the serious amateur groups can have a whole important field of work to themselves. For in all but the wealthier Civic Theatres it will be impossible to present professionally, with any hope of making the production pay for itself, a whole range of fine plays of an unusual and difficult character, beyond the reach of a smallish professional company. And with these plays, many of which will probably be foreign classics, the intelligent and serious amateurs can justify all their claims for themselves. Here is their own special task, of which they can reasonably be proud. They can take their time – as indeed they should do – choosing their play, casting and rehearsing, secure from the challenge of any finance committee. If the play calls for odd types, as it almost certainly will, they can throw a wide net for such types. They can make experiments in staging and lighting without feeling they are annoying the regular customers. And if between such productions, which might be old English, French, Russian, Chinese, they can find a promising first piece by a local writer, who will learn more by seeing his play performed than by posting it to half the managers in England, then these amateur companies will be doing double service to the Theatre and to their community. And their brightest members must not be too openly scornful about the poor toiling professional. For we are trying to create the kind of Theatre in which it ought to be easy to be a bright amateur this year and a hopeful professional next year. The toil will still be there, but it will then glow with a new ardour.

Why Bother?

Some readers may have been asking this question from the beginning: 'Why all this fuss about the Theatre, anyhow? It may be all right for you, who happen to be a dramatist and earn a good part of your living in the Theatre, to denounce our present commercial muddle and chaos and waste of time and effort, to demand that the nation's theatrical life should be properly organised; but why should we, who have more important things to think about, worry about the state of the Theatre? Does it all really matter? And if not – as we suspect – then why bother?'

People are usually too polite to say these things, but often when we are openly fussing about the Theatre we can see these doubts and queries flickering in their eyes. A lot of educational experts and official bigwigs, the types who pounce on the Times crossword puzzle, really think like this. So do most of the politicians. They do not object to an occasional 'amusing show' to unbend their minds, but all this heavy palaver about the Theatre only arouses their suspicion. They feel that those of us who enjoy messing about in theatres are being too solemn and claiming too much for our antics. And what with films, radio, television, all entertaining more and more people, probably the Theatre has had its day. So why bother?

Let me first clear myself of the charge that I am merely another shoemaker crying, 'Nothing like leather!' I did not go to work in the Theatre and then discover, because it helped me to earn a living, that the Theatre is important. I left other kinds of writing, which offered me a safe living and far more peace of mind, to work in the Theatre because I believed the Theatre to be important. And more than once, irritated, bored or depressed by the chaotic conditions and the horrible waste of time and effort, I have told myself that I would write no more for the Theatre, would compete no longer in its nightmare obstacle race, but always I have returned because I have never been able to rid myself of the conviction that the Theatre, representing the communal art of drama, was far more important, far more deeply significant, than most people ever imagined. And as the years rushed towards the Second World War, plunged into its dark gulf, and then began to creep out again towards daylight, I felt that our need of the Theatre was growing and deepening, that this particular art meant far more now than it could have done 50 years ago, at a time of comparative ease and security, and that no matter how appalling the conditions of theatrical production might become

– and they have got steadily worse during my time in the Theatre, and I am one of the least patient of men – I must do what little I could to help. And that is why I am writing this book, of which this final section, faulty though it may be, is perhaps the best part. For here I must try to explain why I consider the Theatre so important, what makes it peculiarly significant, and why our need of it, at a time when there is plenty of other entertainment, is growing and deepening, like a hunger of the soul.

It will not do, although this frequently happens, to praise the Theatre in terms of the literary gifts of the great dramatists. The poetry and sense of character of Shakespeare! The profound social criticism of Ibsen! The tenderness of Chekhov and the wit of Shaw! All very fine and true, but you can enjoy all these, taking your own time, at home, if necessary snugly curled up in bed. The works of all the great dramatists are to be had nicely printed and bound, and with the help of a little imagination you can appreciate much of what these fertile minds have to offer, without sitting for three hours in a crowded and perhaps uncomfortable playhouse. (Many people, of course, really enjoy just sitting in a playhouse, but I am not one of them and I tend to resent this inevitable part of the business.) Naturally, the poetry and wit and wisdom of the great dramatists enter into the picture, and we are at liberty to tell the non-playgoing reader that he is missing much that good directors, actors, designers would offer him in the actual Theatre. But this will not really take us very far. The man who despises or mistrusts the Theatre will not be converted by this mild argument. We have to see the Theatre as something much more than a superior substitute for the reading of dramatic literature. We have to prove that it is valuable and unique, that it does something supremely well worth doing, and that nothing else can take its place.

J B PRIESTLEY

The Work of Art

A theatrical production is itself a work of art of a most curious
and complicated kind. It may be a very bad work of art, and
the odds at present in this country are against its being a
good one, but a work of art it remains. But not because it
may make use of other arts – poetry, music, painting. (This
is the mistake Wagner made when he claimed so much for
his kind of opera, which he imagined to be a super-art because
it asked for poet, musicians, singer-actors, painters. But you
cannot really add the arts together like this. There is always
as much subtraction going on as there is addition.) The art of
drama, as actually presented on the stage, is not a collection
of bits and pieces from the other arts, but another kind of art,
not very pure perhaps, messy and a trifle vulgar no doubt, but
existing in its own right. This is something that many critics
and experienced playgoers do not seem to understand. Thus,
I detect this misunderstanding behind the suggestion,
frequently made, that our Theatre could be raised to a far
higher level of achievement if only our poets would write for
it. But during the 19th century, greater poets than our
contemporary ones, Coleridge, Shelley, Byron, Tennyson,
Browning, Swinburne, did write dramas of a kind, but nothing
came of it. The poet must turn himself into a dramatist,
must contribute to the specific art of drama. I think I enjoy
verbal splendour, music, colour, pageantry, as much as the
next man, and I know that these can enrich drama, but I
know, too, that they cannot create it. The most beautiful
actress in the country, robed as a medieval queen by a superb
designer, who has also done a wonderful set, may offer us a
death scene in which she speaks the most sumptuous rhetoric,
accompanied by music supplied by one of our best composers;
and yet we may feel nothing at all; whereas, at a neighbouring
theatre, against a dingy commonplace setting, a rather ugly
young woman in a dirty mackintosh may mutter an apparently

banal phrase or two, and yet make us feel all the heartbreak of this life and so haunt our imagination for years. In the first theatre we have been offered all the trappings and nothing else, and in the second theatre we have experienced the peculiar art of drama. And its wonder and its beauty are all its own, and must not be confused with other kinds.

In a good theatrical production we are offered a piece of life so shaped and coloured and contrived that everything in it, down to the smallest detail, is significant. In this tiny world, artfully created by the Theatre, chaos and chance and the meaningless have been abolished. The shape and colour of a room, the way the light falls through the window, the choice of furnishings, the very relation between a chair and a stool, all mean something. The moment when a man lights a cigarette, the way in which he lights it, his manner of inhaling and blowing out the smoke, all have their places in the pattern. A sudden laugh, a startled look, a cough, a turn of the head, none of these is accidental and each has its own significance. For two or three hours everything offered to our eyes and ears is exquisitely contrived to achieve meaning and purpose. Now if a god or some infinitely wise being decided to take a sharp look at a group of us for an hour or two, no doubt this is how he would see us. In the Theatre, author and director and players bring together all their knowledge, experience, intuition and imagination, and labour for weeks in one of the most delicate pieces of co-operative effort known to man, in an attempt to make us feel that we enjoy for a little time the profound insight and the searching wisdom of that god. Things are made easy for us, within reasonable limits, but that does not mean we can take it all in if we are half-asleep and yawning or are still preoccupied with our own affairs. The better the production, the more of our undivided attention it will claim, and the sharper will be our delight. I shall never forget the exhilaration I felt when I saw the Moscow Arts Theatre production of *The Cherry Orchard*. The curtain had not been up five minutes when I realised that here was a performance as near perfection as human endeavour could make it, and I felt such a rush of exultation that I could have stood up and shouted for joy. That is the Theatre as it should be, and let no man, no philosopher, scientist, statesman, no matter how great his achievements or how wide his interests may be, tell me that the playhouse with its paint and posturing is not worthy of his attention, for I shall retort that no man on earth is so great and wise that he can afford to ignore experience so searching and moving, lighting up the mind and warming the heart. As for most ordinary folk, who are so often half-asleep or lost in a maze of petty egoism (as indeed most of us are), they may be worthy of better Theatre than is mostly offered them; but they will have to be born again, and know more strenuous and enlightened lives, before they are ready to match, with the quality of their attention, the experience that the Theatre at its best can give them. We have all a long way to go yet before we can pluck out the heart of this mystery.

The Audience

So far we have merely considered the relation between the play and the individual spectator. But the Theatre does not really think in terms of individual spectators, but of a collective spectator – the audience. And a genuine theatrical audience is not simply an assembly of individuals, all reacting as they would in private. Everything is heightened and felt more because in such an audience there is a collective response. And it is here, I think, that we part company with some fastidious minds, who mistrust and fear this collective response and profoundly dislike being overwhelmed by it. But most of these people are, I fancy, consciously or unconsciously influenced by their fear of some hysterical demagogue and potential dictator, and have a Hitler at the back of their minds.

This heightened collective response, this sharing of experience, which has always been an essential part of religious ritual, is something that most of us urgently need from time to time. And we need it far more than our grandfathers did, for they lived in smaller communities, were more snugly interwoven into the fabric of society, and regularly gathered together in places of worship. It is not sufficiently realised even yet how many people, especially in the huge urban areas, feel desperately lonely, rootless, lost. A good deal of that contemporary 'craze for amusement' which is so regularly denounced springs from a desire to be rid of this feeling, to share something with other people. Unfortunately the film, the favourite choice of most of these folk, has nothing like the same unifying and heightening effect upon the spectators that a play has. It has only a mere shadow, being itself a shadow, of the intimate relationship that a play has with its audience. There is, of course, an audience reaction to a film, and a certain collective broadening of the response to humour or pathos. Nevertheless, the people in a cinema are not really an audience in the Theatre sense; they never achieve a kind of collective personality, playing a part; they are not dominated, as Theatre audiences are, by one huge mood; they are just a lot of people who are there to look at photographs and listen to recorded sounds. Notice how we feel miserable in a theatre that is more than half empty, whereas we care nothing if there is nobody in the cinema but ourselves. And no matter how much we enjoy films (and I enjoy them too, and this is not an attack upon films, which have their own definite advantages and points of superiority), we tend soon to forget even the most enjoyable evening of them, but we remember our best nights at the Theatre as long as we live. It is the fashion among younger people now to make up parties to go to the cinema, but the few times that I have been taken along I have found myself staring at the silvered screen, in the impersonal atmosphere of the vast shadow show, with a distinct sense of anti-climax. The Theatre ought to have been our destination.

All these people who do feel desperately lonely, rootless, lost, should try to bring themselves back into the community, and I am certainly not offering playgoing as a substitute for religion, social and political consciousness, neighbourliness, and a real family life. But I do declare that the Theatre, not every night, but at fairly frequent intervals, has far more to offer such people than film-going, listening to the radio, nights with the newest fiction. For if it is good Theatre, it will break down their sense of isolation, by making them share a complicated set of responses with hundreds of other people, with whom they are co-operating – and often in the most elaborate fashion – to play the part of Audience. It has to be good Theatre because bad Theatre does not succeed in creating this part of Audience. And this explains why an indifferent play irritates or bores us far more than an indifferent film. Faced with the latter we lean back and smoke and begin to think about other things. But the indifferent play or the poor production annoys because it fails to do what it promised to do, namely, to make us lose ourselves for the time-being in the collective personality of the audience. But if it really succeeds, then our experience is at once far more stimulating and refreshing and altogether more memorable than anything that happens to us in the cinema or while listening to the radio. And even if we are not the kind of persons who feel lonely, rootless, lost, we shall still benefit by the experience. Our links with our fellows will be strengthened. Some of the strain and stress will have been lifted. We shall be more conscious of our sense of community. That is why the Soviet leaders, faced with the task of creating this sense of community, showed a touch of genius when they did so much to encourage the art of the Theatre. And that is why our own politicians, faced with this same task, seem to some of us so obtuse when they imagine that the commercial chaos of our Theatre is no affair of theirs.

A word or two more about this relation between actors and audience. It is delicately adjusted every night. The audience must play its part, and if – let us say, on a wet Monday – it is feeling depressed or sleepy, then the actors heighten their playing a little, quicken their pace, to brighten up the audience; whereas if it is Saturday night and everybody in front is too lively, the actors modify their performance to quieten it down. A good company knows very soon what will be expected of it. And this adjusting of the relationship to strike the right balance is one of the most delightful accomplishments of good Theatre. For this reason nobody should ever grumble about paying more for a seat in a theatre than for a seat at the cinema. A film cannot make any allowance for any particular audience, cannot adjust itself to the evening's mood, can only come whirring out of its spool; but whenever you see a good company in a theatre you are seeing a performance most exquisitely contrived for you and your fellow members of the audience. On the other hand, you on your side cannot fully enjoy what is happening unless you lose your sense of separation from the people all round you, become part of the audience and indeed part of the whole performance, sharing the collective response and experience. If you refuse to do this, preferring your isolation, then you will inevitably miss much of what the Theatre can offer you, and had better stay away. (For this reason, Special Occasions in the Theatre, when the members of the audience are so conscious of themselves that they remain isolated individuals, rarely show the art of the drama at its best.) This business of actors appearing on platforms before gaping and rather noisy assemblies of people has a long history behind it, and seems to some persons a primitive sort of affair, likely to be banished any day now from the more civilised centres, in favour of stereoscopic talking pictures and television that is laid on like hot and cold water. What such persons do not understand is this wonderful actor-audience relation, which only exists in the living Theatre and cannot find a way into these inventions and shadow shows. That is why the Theatre, old as she is, remains the never-to-be-superseded great mother of all drama and entertainment, the everlasting fount of dramatic experience and inspiration.

The Mystery

I shall write this last section of all for my own pleasure. The reader has been warned. Like most workers in the Theatre, I have gone to my day's task in playhouses during urgent national crises and when air-raid sirens have been sounding and when bombs of various kinds have been actually falling, and there has always been something about that task, some queer inexplicable urgency that had nothing to do with fame, publicity, applause, money, which made me completely forget everything that was happening outside. (I remember once helping to rehearse a company, during an air-raid period, when a night's sleep was not to be had and transport was appalling. Yet three members of that company, whose combined ages made a total of more than 200 years, were there every morning at rehearsal, cheerfully climbing on and off an assortment of boxes and planks that represented our scene. There they were, undaunted, as eager as the youngest understudy, after 50 years of it, mysteriously nourished, kept young and hopeful, defying age and weariness, cynicism and decay. And I remember asking myself then: *What is the secret?*) There is, I swear to you, far more in this queer business than meets the eye. Behind all this tawdry mess of paint and canvas and lights and dog-eared scripts and books of press cuttings and vanity and egoism, there is a mystery. Is it because the Theatre, as Shakespeare and others have told us, is a microcosm of our life? Is there a profound symbolism in this art of drama that haunts the depths of the mind, rooting its fascination into the unconscious, which is itself a mighty Theatre? Does this little dream of the playhouse somehow chime and match with the long dream of man's life? Does it hint at profound truths for which we have never been able to find the right words? Is there in all this business of setting the stage and donning wigs and costumes and raising the curtain on tragedy and comedy some queer suggestion of symbolic ritual? And are there not moments in all our lives, moments both of ecstasy and terror, when suddenly we feel that our time goes by in a vast playhouse of rising suns and waning moons? And when we sleep do not curtains rise on fantastic stages, in secret deeply-hidden playhouses where we appear as audience, dramatists, directors, actors, scene-shifters, and all? We cannot escape from some form of play-acting. Let us then give the Theatre, which we can all share, its proper place in our new democratic society, honour and admire its good work, and watch it brighten in our affection.

1946

'AN INTERNATIONAL DRAMATIST'

IN 1947 my father was Chairman of the International Theatre Conference in Paris, and again in Prague in 1948, first President of the International Theatre Institute, and Chairman of the British Theatre Conference. Of the International Theatre Institute he wrote:

Now I may fairly be called an international dramatist. Some plays of mine have been produced all over the world, from the Arctic Circle to the banks of the Amazon. I never visit other countries merely to see plays of mine, but nevertheless it is a fact that since the war, and quite by chance, I have seen productions of one play alone, *An Inspector Calls*, in Moscow, New York, Paris, Copenhagen, Prague, Vienna; and I know that it has been performed in about eight other capital cities. But although I am clearly entitled to describe myself as an international dramatist, I never feel that I belong to an international Theatre. I feel that if there is such a thing, in this post-war world, as an international Theatre, then I have no real part in it. To myself I am an English dramatist who happens to have many of his plays produced abroad. I learn through my agents where these plays have been produced, and now and again a manager or director will send me photographs, a programme or a playbill. But no manager or director or star actor from abroad ever writes to ask me if I am writing anything suitable for him or to enquire about one of my earlier plays. No doubt my agents have enquiries of this kind, for clearly a lot of business must be transacted in order that all these foreign performances should be given; but although I have met many fine directors and actors through my plays abroad, and have often been delightfully entertained by them, nevertheless, as I sit here at home, planning a play or writing it, I have no sense of belonging to a truly international Theatre, have no feeling that I am one useful unit in a world order of Theatre folk, I have no conviction that I am working all the time with dramatic colleagues from many different lands.

And obviously this is all wrong. And it is one reason why I have long wanted an International Theatre Institute, an organisation that would enable me to feel that I was part of a world order of makers of drama.

I want to know what my colleagues are doing, in so many delightful but distant playhouses. I want them to know what I am doing. If we have any new devices and tricks, I want us to be sharing them. I should like to know what their audiences are like, these days. Are there any new and brilliant leading actors and actresses? Is there anybody I might borrow for a play or a film? Managers and agents are all very well, but I prefer to exchange some kinds of information with fellow artists. Anything new and exciting in scene designing? Or lighting? Who are the promising younger playwrights? Is anybody anywhere solving the problem (perhaps the most urgent theatrical problem of our time) of constructing a theatre that is intimate in its atmosphere and yet holds well over a thousand people? I do not know whether the world needs an International Institute; but I do know that I am badly in need of one.

World Theatre, Introductory Issue, 1950

DRAGON'S MOUTH

ONE OF J B PRIESTLEY's more interesting experiments was to devise and direct a platform production (co-written by Jacquetta Hawkes), as a way of creating a drama which could easily tour with a minimum set-up and so be played in any convenient hall. It proved more difficult than he imagined.

On Easter Saturday afternoon, I found myself climbing into a scarlet motor coach, heavily loaded with lighting and sound equipment and baggage. We were off to Malvern to give our first performance of *Dragon's Mouth*, the 'Dramatic Quartet' that Mrs Jacquetta Hawkes and I had written and I had produced. We were taking to the road, to play one-night stands, barnstormers in the modern style.

We were having an adventure and at the same time making what seemed to me an important dramatic experiment. And both the experiment and the adventure really began last October in New York City.

The exact spot was the pleasant dining-room of the Algonquin Hotel. There I was the guest of my old friend, Sir Cedric Hardwicke. We were dining early, and Sir Cedric was apologetic about this, but explained that he had to cross to Brooklyn to perform, as he had been doing for the past year all across the American Continent, in Charles Laughton's production of Shaw's *Juan in Hell*. 'Why don't you come with me?' he said.

I hesitated, for, to be frank, I felt no desire to attend this performance. I imagined it to be a stunt production designed to exploit film stars. However, I agreed to go, and set out for Brooklyn with Sir Cedric and Charles Boyer.

Although I sharply disagree with much of what Shaw says in *Juan in Hell*, I enjoyed myself enormously in that crowded

Brooklyn auditorium. The production was extremely adroit and the acting first-class, but what captured me at once was the feeling of freshness, zest, attack, that the whole thing had. I felt much closer to the actors than I had ever done in the ordinary Theatre.

These performers in evening clothes, pretending to read and using no scenery, make-up, fancy lighting, brought the piece to life. And it was clear that the whole audience felt this. There was a tremendous and quite unusual liveliness about the occasion. The laughter and applause came far more easily than they do in the ordinary Theatre. And as soon as the last word had been spoken on the platform, I hurried backstage to congratulate Charles Laughton and to tell him what I had been feeling about his experiment.

He gave me one of his huge grins. Then he told me that they had to go away again for two or three weeks but after that would be opening at the Century Theatre, New York, for a short run. I told him he would find me there. And then the pair of us, two stout Yorkshiremen, exchanged a knowing look.

It was after one of the performances at the Century Theatre that I ran into Mrs Jacquetta Hawkes, she returning from visits to Harvard and Yale. (We had been staunch allies in our UNESCO days, when Mrs Hawkes was still at the Ministry of Information.)

She had felt much the same as I had about this production of *Juan in Hell*, and when I told her that I believed there was somewhere here the basis of a new form of dramatic writing, she instantly agreed.

I had already said as much to Charles Laughton, who then informed me that he had been hoping all along that I would make this discovery for myself, because he felt that I might then try my hand at writing something that he could produce in more or less the same style, on a platform, without sets, costumes, and the usual theatrical effects. He and I had several discussions about it all (and by this time I had lost interest in the ordinary Theatre job I had originally gone out there to do), at the same time Mrs Hawkes agreed to collaborate with me and after several meetings we had sketched out the dramatic background and the characters of *Dragon's Mouth*.

Back in London, after Christmas, my collaborator and I exchanged visits between Regents Park (where she lives) and Albany (where I live) and worked hard and fast on the exciting new job. Some of the long speeches are entirely hers, and some are entirely mine, and the rest of the piece is a rather cunning mixture of our very different talents. (Two of the characters in *Dragon's Mouth* are men, two are women, but – critics, please note – we did not assign these characters to ourselves according to our respective sex.)

At last the piece was done and a copy was air-mailed to Charles Laughton and his business partner, Paul Gregory, and both of them cabled enthusiastic messages about it. With the result that *Dragon's Mouth* was acquired for production in America – I hope early in the autumn.

Meanwhile, I felt that it ought to be done here, and as soon as possible. I had many good reasons for feeling this, although I think the most important reason was that I was desperately eager to try my hand at producing the piece. After having had about 25 ordinary stage plays produced, I was feeling a little stale and needed a brand-new experiment, something to challenge my wits. (Impatience is an old fault of mine, and the passing years show me little improvement.) What I needed badly was an impresario, an eager but efficient showman, who would leave me free to concentrate on the actual production and would take upon himself all the organisation of a provincial tour and afterwards a London run.

But when I need one of these fellows, they never show up (they are far easier to find in New York than they are in London), so we had to make a start without one, doing everything ourselves from scratch – the hard way.

I will admit that these 'platform dramas', which are not played for a week in provincial theatres, but for one night or two in town halls and concert halls, need far more organisation, particularly in the matter of advance publicity and the arrangements for the sale of tickets, than we could give at such short notice to our production of *Dragon's Mouth*. Just as they have to be written, produced, acted, in a new way, so, too, they have to be sold to the public in a new way, belonging as they do neither to the ordinary Theatre nor to the concert or lecture worlds. And it is here – and not, in my view, artistically, dramatically – that the experiment can fail, especially as good organisers are hard to find and the English are apt to be suspicious of, rather than enthusiastic about, anything strangely new.

If any man wants to know what hard work is, let him try rehearsing a *Dragon's Mouth* all day, even with a cast as clever and quick as Dulcie and Michael Denison, Rosamund John and Norman Woolland, and grappling early in the morning and late at night with all the problems of organisation.

For example – just one item – I was haunted for weeks by the idea of a bus with an emergency door at the back, enabling it to be easily loaded. 'There are no buses with doors at the back.' I was told, over and over again. 'There must be,' I retorted. 'I've see hundreds of 'em.' And the day when we must go on the road rapidly drew nearer, and still no back-loading bus, so that I would wake at odd hours of the night and remember that we still had no transport, and all the time our equipment was piling up and beginning to look as if it would weigh tons. Actually, we never did acquire a bus with a door at the back (apparently there is now a rule against it) but managed to adapt this scarlet motor-coach for our purposes.

Another nightmare was this Sunday business. There is no solid reason why *Dragon's Mouth*, which has no sets, costumes, make-up, or ordinary stage tricks, should not be performed on Sunday. But almost at the last minute a local authority, without reading the script, would decide that it would not do to allow this piece to be performed, and then the tour, all one-night stands, would have to be hastily and desperately rearranged, with the result that we were in and out of some towns before most people knew we had been there.

It is really a three-month job organising such a tour, so that everybody knows about it and all who want to buy tickets know where to find them. My publishers, who joined me in the venture, were aware of this fact and were much wiser than I am; but then, it is easy to be wiser than I am when I am hotly impatient to be doing something new.

Sometimes I wondered what my stage staff thought about me and my experiment once they were committed to it on the road. For they really had what is commonly referred to as 'a packet'. First, they would have to travel from – let us say – Coalcastle to Coketown, perhaps a hundred miles or so, in a heavily-loaded coach, groaning and banging and swaying. They would probably arrive at Coketown just too late for lunch, and would go to the hall, which might be anything from a vast town auditorium holding 3,000 people to a Methodist chapel hall, out of a mid-Victorian novel, situated in a back street and with almost no facilities of any kind.

They would then have to set up the elaborate sound equipment, the lights, and do what they could with the platform, all of which would take a couple of hours' hard work. By the time they had had some tea, and found where they were going to sleep, the evening performance would be looming. Then, after doing their duty throughout the performance, they would have to take everything down and load the coach, ready for an early start in the morning. *Dragon's Mouth* indeed! I hate to imagine what they thought of me sometimes.

We had all kinds of moments except dull moments. There were ticket agents who were keen about us, but complained that all our arrangements were disastrous – tickets late, not enough bills, wrong advertising. There were other ticket agents who apparently did not care if we dropped dead, and some we never even saw. There were journalists who came to praise us and others who came to knife us. There were photographers who always arrived just when we could not do with them. There were sober municipal bigwigs who did not know what we were trying to do, and tiddly types who suggested late-night binges. There were people who thought we were giving a concert or showing a film, and others who concluded that we were merely out of our minds.

Sometimes the coach missed the right turning, went roaring and swaying along third-class roads, and made all the ladies of the company feel sick. There were late arrivals at hotels that could not take us and at other hotels that we could not take. We always seemed to be eating too much – having a huge Mayor's tea just after a late lunch – or going so hungry that we began to feel faint.

Sometimes we felt bang on top of the world and at other times were sure we were dropping through the bottom of it. We never had any address (or any laundry) and lived in a horrible world of trunk calls and telegrams.

There were, too, the usual forgotten factors. Let me indicate one of them. In my haste I had overlooked the fact that just after our tour was under way, the time would be advanced an hour. This meant that it would still be broad daylight at about the time we were starting our performance. And it had not occurred to me, used as I am to theatres, that most of these halls we had booked or were ready to book had rows of large windows that could not be blacked out. Clearly, the autumn and winter were the seasons for us and not the spring, for although we dispensed with much that belonged to the Theatre we had to have artificial lighting.

Early May would not be too good, and late May would be hopeless, outside a theatre. So we cancelled the later bookings of the projected tour and found ourselves a theatre – the Winter Garden in Drury Lane.

Nevertheless, though we may have made asses of ourselves in half a dozen different ways (for which I will take most responsibility), one glorious shining fact emerged. The dramatic experiment itself was succeeding, perhaps beyond our best expectations. I do not know what will happen to *Dragon's Mouth* in London, where there is so much dependence (far too much, in my view) now on press opinion, but I can state with the utmost sincerity that with the audiences I saw and heard this production succeeded as I had hoped it would succeed.

We fired a shot into the dark – and – wollop! – there was the target. For people listened with an intentness rarely felt in the Theatre. The storms of coughing that accompany most rather long and thoughtful speeches in the average playhouse had been banished. When a witty stroke was made, they laughed appreciatively. Great rounds of applause greeted the end of many of the longer speeches. Without most of the usual theatrical devices and aids, the piece seized and held their imagination.

I realised that they felt closer, as I had hoped they would, to the characters and their dramatic situation and their various revelations, than they did in the familiar Theatre. They responded directly and with warmth to the appeal of the actors, whose personalities seemed more sharply revealed than they customarily do. The audience, in fact, was more a part of the production. Depending as we did on ideas and words and the direct appeal of the performers, and hardly at all on visual effects, we had made some sort of return to the satisfying manner of Classical and Elizabethan Drama.

I must not encourage myself to make rash prophecies. I will only say this. I realise that this new form is not easy to write well, is hard to produce and act properly, and needs a great deal of efficient organising, together with much enthusiasm on the part of everybody concerned with it. I have never regarded it as a challenge to the ordinary Theatre, and merely see it as another approach to the art of dramatic entertainment. The thing may be a flop. (And if it is, I shall tell myself firmly that we are a tired, stale people who need something new, but have not sufficient energy to demand it and then welcome it.)

But here is a way of performing pieces that are better vehicles for ideas and heightened oratorical speeches than conventional plays are, and the method of presentation is so flexible that 4,000 people in a concert hall could enjoy such pieces, if they are sufficiently well written and produced, and fifty people could equally enjoy them in a village institute.

And it seems to me that our age, menaced as it is by the vast standardisation and monopoly of TV, and lacking as it is in playhouses for the smaller towns, stands in peculiar need of such a flexible form, just as its people, our people, in fact, you and I, stand in need of the stimulation of ideas, the emotional force of good writing and powerful acting, and, indeed, all that the drama in any form can give us.

'The Story of *Dragon's Mouth*', *Everybody's*, 24 May 1952

THE ART OF THE DRAMATIST

ORIGINALLY a lecture followed by a question and answer session at the Old Vic Theatre in 1956, 'The Art of the Dramatist' was published by Heinemann the following year. My father later reworked and revised the text as a radio talk in four parts, and this duly appeared in The Listener; *I have mostly drawn on the latter, with some elements from his follow-up added to the main text in the slim volume. It combines his fascinating theory of 'dramatic experience' with more practical hints on the technique of writing drama.*

The Nature of the Drama

Why do we go to the Theatre? What is it we enjoy there? If we go to follow the fortunes of imaginary characters, why do we trouble ourselves about the actors? If we go to enjoy the actors, why should the quality of the play worry us? Working in the Theatre for a quarter of a century, I had often considered these and similar questions, until finally I evolved a theory of the drama that seemed to me to answer them all. I made this theory the subject of lectures at universities in many different countries, and at places like the Old Vic in London, the *Beaux Arts* in Brussels, the *Kammerspiele* in Vienna. If this theory of the drama has been kicking about for generations in various books and periodicals, all I can say is that I have never come across any of them, and that although I make no pretence of scholarly research, and so could easily be wrong, I believe it to be a new and original theory.

Coleridge, in his introduction to his lectures on Shakespeare, discusses the nature of drama, and he seems to me to come much closer to understanding it than anybody before him. He sees that it is equally wrong to insist upon stage-illusion as actual delusion (a fault he attributes to French criticism) or to deny it altogether, as Dr Johnson did. He

174

declares that the mind voluntarily accepts stage-illusion by refusing to judge that it is false. We take to the Theatre what he calls 'a willing suspension of disbelief'. With disbelief suspended, with no time to ask questions or pass judgements, we are then, he tells us, taken by storm – or, as we might say, we are bounced into accepting what we see and hear. Coleridge tells us that, 'What would appear mad or ludicrous in a book, when presented to the sense under the form of reality, and with the truth of nature, supplies a species of actual experience.' And this is really as far as he can go. It is not far enough.

Coleridge avoids the traps into which the 18th-century critics fell. He is safely out in the open but he will not boldly press on. When he has arrived at the term 'experience' his goal is in sight, but he hangs back, is content as a theorist to be merely negative. So he does not really explain why we feel our experience in the Theatre to be different from other kinds of experience. After all, many things take us by storm; and even a willing suspension of disbelief is not uniquely associated with the Theatre. We suspend our disbelief when we are reading a fairy story or fantasy or listening with pleasure to somebody telling a tall story. Had he spent more time in the Theatre, Coleridge would have realised that it makes a far more positive contribution than he supposed, that our response on the level of dramatic convention and technique, our consciousness of assisting in a theatrical presentation, our relation with the actors, are as necessary to the complete experience as our imaginative sympathy with the personages and life of the play. In other words – and here we arrive at my own theory – we go to the Theatre to enjoy a special kind of experience, which we can reasonably call 'dramatic experience', and this experience is created by our response on two different levels at the same time. Or allow me to put it like this: the bull has two horns; Coleridge's French critics were impaled on one of them, Dr Johnson on the other; Coleridge saw the danger and so he dithered between them; but now we must grasp each horn firmly – and take home the beef!

Let us try out the theory. I say there is something I call 'dramatic experience', a very special kind of experience, arrived at in a unique way, and that without this experience the Theatre cannot be understood and enjoyed. Now as both a father and a grandfather on a fairly substantial scale, I have in my time often taken young children to the Theatre. What happens? If they are too small, not old enough to enjoy dramatic experience, they simply feel they are in a large strange place where something real is happening, and either they are frightened, because what is happening seems strange and menacing, or they are bored and want to explore the nearest aisle and clutch, with chocolate-sticky fingers, the trousers of neighbouring gentlemen. A year or two later these same children may be a wonderful audience, entranced and entrancing.

What has happened? They have arrived at dramatic experience. And, if we assume that the piece being performed is suitable for children, we can say that this experience has for them an unusual intensity, often a glory and a magic difficult to recapture in later life, just because they are fully and eagerly responsive on both our necessary levels. For they are rapturously concerned with the characters and action of the piece being presented, but at the same time they are more intensely conscious than adults are of not being physically involved in the scene, of sitting in the plush seats safely and snugly by the side of Mummy or kind Uncle William. So two wonderful things are happening at once; and I cannot help feeling that it is the child surviving in us who makes us fully responsive to the Theatre. I have noticed that men and women who are completely removed from their childhood, who are finally and rather awfully adult so that it is impossible to imagine them as children, generally dislike the Theatre and are reluctant and unresponsive playgoers.

I am not clever enough to explain exactly what happens in our minds when we are enjoying dramatic experience, but at least I am clever enough not to make any attempt. A full-scale attempt would demand the combined efforts of half the members of the British Association. I do not know – and to be honest, do not care – if we respond on these two different levels of the mind actually at the same time, really simultaneously, or if we alternate between them, flashing from one to the other at a very high speed. My concern here is not the working of the human mind and the structure of the brain – but the art of the drama. And I am certain that there is this double response, and that creates a unique type of experience. Try to work out the attraction of the Theatre in terms of a single response, and you are in trouble at once.

Let us take a simple example, and suppose we are watching an old-fashioned melodrama. The beautiful innocent heroine, her golden hair in pretty disorder, is in a situation of appalling danger – tied to a railway line, about to be fed to a circular saw, bound hand and foot, and entirely at the mercy of the king of the underworld. We sit there, making no attempt to rush forward and rescue her. Why should we? We know she is not a beautiful innocent girl in danger but the wife of the touring manager, wearing a rather tatty wig, that there is no approaching train, real circular saw, and that the terrible king of the underworld is an oldish actor whom we noticed drinking a bitter at lunchtime in the White Lion. So it is all nothing, a lot of rubbishy pretence. Very well. Then why do we still sit there, instead of going for a walk or having a drink; and not only sit there, perhaps enduring much discomfort, but lean forward and stare hard and perhaps hold our breath, and then break into applause when the heroine is rescued in the nick of time? We must be out of our minds. And that is true, for once we are in the Theatre and enjoying dramatic experience, we are out of our ordinary minds. You might say we are deliberately schizophrenic. We pay money to split ourselves in two. One part of us is living desperately with the innocent heroine and the terrible king of the underworld, while the other part is sitting cosily in the stalls of the Theatre Royal Coketown, enjoying this week's show.

I maintain that everybody and everything in the Theatre has this double character; they are seen in the strange light and shadow of belief and disbelief; they belong to a heightened reality that we feel deeply and yet know to be unreal. (And incidentally, something like this seems to happen to us in moments of great danger, when reality itself suddenly turns into a kind of dramatic experience, as if the whole world were a giant theatre and all this life a drama, so much play-acting compared with some unknown deeper reality.) It is this experience, unlike any other – with the exception I have sketched out in parenthesis – that I call 'dramatic experience', and the Theatre exists to provide it for us.

So it is in the delicate relation between belief and disbelief, between the dream life of the play and the real life in the play's presentation, between the stage as a window upon and an entrance into imaginary existences and the stage as an exhibition of highly technical skills, that our true dramatic experience has its roots and its being. I call this realism 'delicate' because the necessary balance is easily disturbed, and when it is disturbed the experience loses its unique quality, its character changes, its colours fade. If what happens on one level of the mind completely dominates the situation, so that what happens on the other level is hardly attended to, there is no true dramatic experience.

For example, if I go to the Theatre in my professional capacity, to look at a certain actor with a part for him in mind, to discover if the new lighting system they are using is working well, to admire the work of the scene designer, I put myself outside true dramatic experience. Its magic does not work for me, just because there is no double response, for I am not responding at all on one necessary level. This is obvious. What is not so obvious, though it is equally true, is that we are still outside dramatic experience, have missed the magic, if we forget we are in a theatre at all, if we are completely lost in the imaginary life of the play, like the good lady who during the performance of *Othello*, outraged by the Moor's jealous suspicion, jumped up and shouted: 'You big black fool – can't you *see*?' This is harder to understand, if only because it is often held that this complete deception, audiences carried away like those in the old mining camps of California and Nevada who would rush the stage to rescue the heroine, represents the drama's ultimate triumph, what we have all been aiming at. But this is wrong. These naive spectators may have had an uproariously good evening, all the better when they ceased to be spectators and joined in, but it would not have been an evening illuminated by dramatic experience. The crucial inner relation between play and reality would not have been achieved. If you doubt this, then ask yourself if, wanting a responsible and sensitive appreciation of that particular production of *Othello*, you would have gone first to the lady who shouted at the Moor. Of course not. Like the gold miners storming the stage, she was not in the Theatre, that lady. But Othello *is* in the Theatre, *of* the Theatre, belonging essentially *to* the Theatre.

Analogies between the arts are always tricky, but I think we might risk one here. An essential element in the true appreciation of painting is the enjoyment of pigments on canvas. We have to be thoroughly alive to the fact that the artist is using paint. A picture may reveal to us an extraordinary mind and temperament, it may communicate a unique vision of this world, but it can only do these and other things through our feeling for form and colour expressed in paint. No paint, no pictorial art. Here the paint roughly represents what the Theatre contributes to the art of the drama. It indicates one of the two levels on which we must respond. No Theatre, no art of the drama. Reading a play to oneself may be enjoyable, especially to people familiar with the Theatre, but there will be no true dramatic experience.

There is some confusion here because many great dramatists, such as Shakespeare, have given us work of a high literary value, work that is enchanting simply to read, lines that are bewitching as poetry. Nevertheless, we must make a distinction between Shakespeare the poet, whom we read, and Shakespeare the dramatist, the creator of dramatic experience, who can only be properly appreciated in the Theatre. And it is a mistake, in my opinion, to suppose, as so many people do, that the poet in him is always entirely at the service of the dramatist, for there are times when the poet cannot resist making a character say some splendid flashing thing that is entirely out of key with that particular character, so making us feel that the dramatist has temporarily been defeated.

Again, we may prefer, as I do, reading some scenes to seeing and hearing them in the playhouse, but this is simply because their beauty as literature happens to mean more to us than any dramatic experience they can create for us in the Theatre. But the fact remains that Shakespeare the dramatist, like any other dramatist, has to be discovered where he belongs, in the Theatre busy with his players creating dramatic experience for us. And here let me add that because our greatest poet and our greatest dramatist happen to be the same astonishing genius, Shakespeare, there have been endless muddles and confusion, here in England, in our consideration of the drama. For example, the familiar notion that if we can persuade our poets to write for the Theatre, they will somehow turn themselves into great dramatists just because Shakespeare did; though in point of fact nearly all our major poets during the 19th century did write plays but contributed little of lasting value to the Theatre.

It is here that our theory of 'dramatic experience', based on a response on two different levels of the mind, begins to justify its existence. For I believe it can provide us with valuable insights, help us to avoid many common mistakes about the Theatre, to separate sense from nonsense in much dramatic criticism and theorising, find a way for us through what appear to be trackless swamps and jungles. But let us be clear first about this double response. We must understand what it involves. An audience, if it is behaving as an audience should behave, if in fact it is enjoying true dramatic experience, the unique kind of experience the Theatre exists to create, is at one and the same time lost in the imaginary life of the play and yet aware, often intensely aware, of what is actually happening, namely the presentation in terms of the Theatre of that life. It is seeing and hearing both Prospero and Sir John Gielgud, Imogen and Dame Peggy Ashcroft. It is, so to speak, this successful focusing of the mind that gives the experience delight and depth. It is not like life – seeing Hamlet die is quite different from seeing a man die outside in the street – and yet it is far from being idle mummery, for we have to *feel* Hamlet's death. And some kind of balance between these two responses is undoubtedly involved, and if this balance is upset, if there is too much of one, too much of the other, the true experience is missed.

What follows from this? A good deal, unless I have been merely boasting about how the theory can help us. For example, if, as I maintain, we are always aware of the Theatre and its essential to the experience that we should be, then it is reasonable to believe that the difference between various kinds of Theatre, various ways of writing, producing and acting, is a mere matter of convention and taste. You may, of course, prefer one to another; one convention may be rather stale while another may seem fresh, novel, stimulating; you have a right to your personal preferences; but, if this theory is correct, you must not declare, as so many people do, that one kind of Theatre, one way of writing, producing and acting, succeeds in creating the experience when all others fail.

All drama rests upon convention. What is called 'realism' or 'naturalism' in the Theatre may now, as some critics tell us, be a stale convention, its innumerable small fussy effects may seem tedious or irritating. Fair enough, as people say. But it simply will not do to tell us that what is wrong with realism is that it persuades people that they are not in a Theatre. They do not mistake the set in Act Two for a real solicitor's office. If they did, they would have no dramatic experience. Again, some modern dramatists and directors, reacting against realism, tell us we must be reminded we are in the Theatre, that everything said and done must be 'theatrical', which generally means that characters have red circles painted on their cheeks and jerk about like puppets. This may or may not be a useful and amusing new convention, a change from those solicitors' offices with every detail right; I am not arguing that, one way or the other; what I am saying is that the alleged reason for this change of convention – to remind people they are in the Theatre – is nonsense, because people do not need reminding. Let us have different conventions by all means – I like experiment in the Theatre – but it is not necessary to explain them by writing and talking nonsense, to cover the absurdly arrogant claim that one convention alone can offer audiences the experience they demand.

Let us now see how the theory can guide us in another direction. Do we go to the Theatre to pass an evening agreeably, to be amused, or do we go to learn something, to receive the author's 'message'? There has been endless debate on this subject, and the questions it asks can never be properly answered because they themselves are not properly stated. We go to the Theatre primarily to enjoy a kind of experience not to be found elsewhere. I am not prepared to say here and now exactly what is the value of this unique experience, where its significance lies, but if you will allow me to do a little guessing, I will suggest that the double response it demands brings some relief – and at the same time a kind of life – to the mind, that its odd combination of attachment and detachment acts in some way as a release, that it brings with it the feeling, all too brief and not at all strong, of living on a higher level of being. When we see a fine production of a good play – and the finer the production and the better the play the greater is our sense of exhilaration – we seem to be raised above the common level of our traffic with our fellow creatures, removed from our usual involvement with them, so that we look and listen as benevolent demi-gods might do, attached through sympathy to the human race, and yet at the same time detached from it, not being involved in its actions.

This may be fanciful but any playgoer who has had any luck at all can doubt the value of the experience. And for this we go to the Theatre. Here is our primary reason. How we interpret the experience, what it does to us, will depend on the character and quality of the play and the production and also on our mood and temperament. Whatever the play is, whether it is *Oedipus* or *Getting Gertie's Garter*, its performance will still demand from the audience this response on two different levels, and must keep the right balance between them to succeed as a performance, but, of course, the quality, the colour and tone, so to speak, of the dramatic experience can vary enormously.

But let us think of the Theatre in terms of this experience, a mixed and highly complicated thing, and not in terms of emotion and thought. No matter what the dramatist writes or how the director and his players interpret what has been written, I cannot believe – as I am told the late Bertolt Brecht believed – that the drama can become the vehicle of pure thought. Anybody in search of pure thought will be well advised not to sit in a building with a thousand other people, a large company of actors, and an orchestra. The conditions could hardly be worse. Better try a lecture room, a library, or a quiet corner at home. Even a Bernard Shaw, our one genius in the drama of debate, is far better able to communicate his ideas directly in his prefaces than in his plays.

I do not mean by this that dramatists should have no ideas, that they themselves should not be thoughtful men. What I am saying is that the drama is not the medium for their direct communication, and that, in fact, we do not go to the Theatre primarily in search of ideas or to be told what to think. What we enjoy there is a particular kind of experience, and if a dramatist cannot create that experience for us, then even if he should be the wisest man alive when he is outside the Theatre, he will have failed inside it. But if he does give us the experience we demand from him, if he is nobly thoughtful, if he sparkles and crackles with brilliant ideas, the experience will be illuminated, heightened, deepened, by what he has first brought to its creation. If a dramatist is also a poet, or a philosopher, or an acute social critic, then so much the better for the dramatic experience we enjoy in his Theatre, but he must be a dramatist first or there is nothing we can enjoy in his Theatre, not even his poetry, his philosophy, his social criticism. The writer who cannot come to terms with the Theatre – and later we shall discover what that involves – is not a dramatist at all, just as a man who does not know what to do with paint and canvas cannot be described as a painter. No Theatre, no dramatic experience. No dramatic experience, no dramatist nor drama. And in my next talk, I will try to examine, in the light of this theory, the dramatist at work.

The Listener, 5 December 1957

The Dramatist and his Work

In my previous talk, on the nature of the drama, I declared that the Theatre exists primarily to provide us with a unique kind of experience that I called 'dramatic experience', and this demanded from us, as audience, a response on two different levels of the mind, one concerned with the imaginary life of the play and its personages, the other with the actual theatrical presentation of that play and its personages. So, I said, we go to see Prospero and Sir John Gielgud, Imogen and Dame Peggy Ashcroft; about which there will be more in my next talk, when I arrive at the dramatist's colleagues, the players. But now we come to the dramatist himself, and here again, as before in our general consideration of the drama, I believe this theory of 'dramatic experience' will give us some insight into a complicated subject and help us to avoid some common mistakes.

We can begin by asking ourselves a familiar question, far more often asked than answered. It is this:

Why are good plays so hard to write?

Perhaps you do not believe they are. If so, then either you are a great find for the English Theatre, which badly needs your genius, or you can never have tried to write plays. At first sight, plays would seem easier to write than – let us say – novels. To begin with, they are generally much shorter, which appears to be a notable advantage. They are written entirely in dialogue and so do not demand an effective and pleasing narrative prose style. As a rule they present far fewer characters than an ordinary novel does. It would seem, too, that the playwright does not need as much general knowledge of life as a novelist does. Again, he does not do everything by himself as the novelist does, for he has directors, scene designers and painters, lighting experts, and beautiful actresses and clever actors, all working for him. So at first sight he appears to have all the advantages. Yet the fact remains that good plays are very hard to write. And horribly bad, impossible plays are all too easy to write. I have in fact been astonished over and over again by the way in which writers distinguished in other forms, good poets or novelists or essayists, can cheerfully submit attempts at play-writing that are appallingly silly. It is as if clever writers could lose all judgement when they approach the Theatre. Perhaps its so-called glamour goes to their heads.

Let us take a closer and more searching look at the novelist and the dramatist. The novelist may have to do it all himself, but generally he does it for one reader at a time, a reader who is devoting himself to the novelist's work at the most appropriate hour, when all his or her sympathies are willing to be engaged. The dramatist, on the other hand, has to hold the attention of his audiences between certain fixed times. They have to take it or leave it, unlike novel readers who can put their books aside when they are bored or want to do something else. The fact that a play compels us to sit there attending to it means that we are far more irritated by it if we cannot respond to it properly. This explains why dramatic critics are generally more bad-tempered and abusive than book reviewers. There is, too, a certain growing fatigue in our attention, so that if a play has a poor last act, we tend to condemn the whole piece. If novels were as harshly judged, if their closing chapters had to be even better than their opening chapters, many works of fiction that now pass as masterpieces would have been condemned as failures. Finally – and this is a most important point – in the prevailing conditions of our Theatre, the dramatist cannot select his audiences as the novelist does and cannot help doing. The dramatist has to hold the attention of perhaps a thousand people at the same time, and they are a thousand very different people, so that what may be boringly obvious to the scientist or lawyer in the stalls may be bewilderingly difficult to the housewife in the dress circle and the greengrocer in the gallery. So any dramatist attempting an unusual theme, which asks for some exposition, soon runs headlong into some tricky problems.

The dramatist's chief difficulty, about which the novelist knows nothing, arises from the fact that he must provide his audiences with this double-impact experience received on two different levels of the mind at the same time. In order to do this successfully – and unless he does it he will fail in the Theatre – the dramatist himself, right from the first, must do a double job, on two levels more or less at the same time. If he fails on one level or the other, if he cannot establish a true balance between them, then the experience ultimately demanded by his audience will be faulty, unsatisfactory, unrewarding. And it is this above all that makes good plays so hard to write. Usually one level or the other is neglected or going wrong; both cylinders are not firing. Just as the audience must receive the play both in terms of its imaginative life and in terms of its theatrical presentation, both as life and as Theatre, so the dramatist must conceive and create his play, from the beginning, in both these terms. So everything for him has a double aspect. And I do not hesitate to add here that the born dramatist is the writer who welcomes rather than resents this double aspect, who finds himself, almost without taking thought, working easily on these two levels at once.

For example, let us suppose the dramatist is working in the familiar theatrical convention of our time, writing a play about the Jones family in Kensington. This family consists of father, mother, daughter, son. These four people must take on life in his imagination. He must know all about them, must live for the time being their life in Kensington. This is one man who really must keep up with the Joneses. But so far he is doing no more than a conscientious novelist must do, and indeed on this level he need not do as much as the novelist must do, for he will not in fact show us as much of the Joneses as we would find in a good novel about them. But this is only half the task of the dramatist, who is writing not to be read but to be performed in a Theatre. He has also to function properly on the other level, that of the Theatre. So while he lives intensely with these four members of the Jones family, he has also to be sharply aware of the two actors and the two actresses for whom he is writing parts. He is not only creating characters, he is also shaping and colouring four actable parts. While one half of his mind is in the Jones sitting room in Kensington, the other half is working with a box set with two practicable doors erected on a stage. Alongside the exciting problems of the Jones family is another and quite different set of problems, concerned not with middle-class London life but with the elaborate techniques of theatrical performance. So everything, I repeat, has this double aspect.

We can now understand what is wrong with so many plays, both plays in manuscript and some that reach the stage. If the writer thinks he need only concern himself with the Jones family and their fortunes, he will go wrong, because, as we have seen, audiences themselves are not completely involved with the Joneses but depend for their experience on a balance between two levels, one of which does not belong to the Joneses but to the Theatre. This explains why many fine poets or brilliant novelists have failed as dramatists; they could not adequately undertake the double duty. But it also explains why very often the artful and experienced Theatre man, who knows all the tricks, fails to write anything worth our time and money. For he works too hard on one level, that of theatrical presentation, to the neglect of the other, on which the Joneses have their being, the level of imaginative life; so that his work seems stale, brittle, false, does not create true dramatic experience for us. We may simplify the matter here by declaring that true drama is created by bringing life to the Theatre, and the Theatre to life. And this is hard to achieve. It is rarely possible to be equally satisfying on each level; as character, action, life, on the one hand, and as the highly conventional art of the Theatre, on the other. And unless the dramatist goes to work like an organist playing on two keyboards at once, the audience cannot respond as it wishes to respond.

This is true no matter what sort of play the dramatist is writing. It is a mistake – and one all too often made – to imagine that a change of theatrical convention, a new style, a different sort of stage, will release us from this basic difficulty. The balance is still essential, the dramatist must still work double, if instead of writing about the Joneses in Kensington he is writing about Cleopatra, Robin Hood, or the captain of the first spaceship, if the Jones' sitting room has been turned into white steps and cylinders against a black curtain; whether the Joneses speak in sloppy realistic prose, or in that rather dubious mixture of knockabout slang and purple passages we find now in so many American plays, or in rhymed couplets or Shakespearean blank verse or the much blanker verse favoured by contemporary poetic dramatists.

Remember, I am only saying that the dramatist cannot escape his basic responsibility merely by a change of convention. What I am *not* saying is that it does not matter what convention he chooses. That is something quite different. His choice will be dictated by his temperament, particular skills and preferences and prejudices, and by what he believes his audience capable of understanding. Clearly if the audience does not understand a certain kind of Theatre, then that kind of Theatre does not exist as a convention for that audience. A Japanese might write a *No* play about the Jones family that had astonishing insight into their characters and relationships, but an ordinary Western audience would be either too bewildered or too amused to achieve the right response. On the other hand, a skilful dramatist may be able to make a little bridge between two quite different conventions as Thornton Wilder did in *Our Town*, in which he makes effective use of certain features of the classical Chinese Theatre in a play intended for Western audiences. We could do with more of these experiments, in which two different theatrical conventions are used to produce another, different from either.

The contemporary dramatist has many difficulties to face unknown to dramatists in other periods, notably the challenge of film and television, the drift away from the Theatre in many sections of the public, the recent steep rise in costs. But the contemporary dramatist has at least one advantage, he is no longer the servant of one particular convention, as he would have been fifty years ago. He can write in verse or prose; if he does not like the picture-frame stage, he can break out of it; if he is tired of realism, he can try his hand at expressionism, symbolism, surrealism; and whatever he decides to do, if he does it boldly and with conviction, he will probably find directors and players ready to interpret his work.

I am not pretending there are no difficulties here. If he is an English dramatist, he will soon discover there are very few recognised playhouses adapted for experimental work. We are badly short of these, for, unlike people on the Continent or in America, we seem now to lack the will or capacity or both to build theatres, even though the far more elaborate and costly erection of television transmitting stations does not seem too much for us. But it is significant – and much to the point here – that the new playhouse planned by an enterprising amateur group in West London will have a stage so contrived that it is not tied to any particular convention; and in this respect it might serve as a pattern and example to all builders of new theatres, if there are to be any more. And there ought to be, of course, even if the public prefers film and television, simply because the live Theatre is still both parent and nurse of all dramatic entertainment, for it is in the live Theatre, and only there, that authors, directors, players, face the audience waiting to enjoy our unique experience.

Let us return to the dramatist who is busy with his play about the Jones family. We have seen that he will have to work on two levels of the mind more or less simultaneously. On one of these, as we know, he is entirely concerned with these Joneses, their characters, their relationships, their varying fortunes, and with this we have nothing to do, except to add that he cannot know too much about the Joneses. Indeed, in order to be able to write one good play about them, he ought to know enough to write ten plays about them. It is both this breadth and depth of knowledge that are clearly absent from plays that are unsatisfactory, though well contrived. But the relation between the dramatist and his Joneses is not our business here. What immediately concerns us is his work on the other level, that of theatrical presentation. As we have seen, he can choose one of several theatrical conventions to work in, an advantage he has over dramatists in most previous ages. But we must not imagine him, if he is a good dramatist, collecting, so to speak, a lot of Jones material and then deciding what dramatic form he will give it. Good plays are never written like that. He will see the Jones family from the beginning in terms of the particular convention, form, style, he prefers to use. The dramatist does not press a lot of human stuff into a dramatic mould. His matter and form have a reciprocal dynamic relationship, like that, we imagine of body and soul. He is creating character at the very moment he is also writing parts for his actors and actresses. There is a two-way traffic between the two levels, between the imaginary and imaginative life within the play and the theatrical presentation of that life, what belongs to the stage; so that, as I said before, life is brought to the Theatre, and the Theatre brought to life.

It is, I think, difficult for people who do not work in the Theatre to understand this two-way traffic; they imagine it is all one-way, from life to the Theatre, from the Joneses to what will happen on the stage. But I am sure any good dramatist will agree with me that successful creation is never one-way like this, that it represents a co-operation, or a two-way traffic, between both levels; so that while, as anybody can see, a relationship between two characters can suggest a stage situation, it is also true that a stage situation can uncover a relationship between two characters. In short, the true dramatist cannot help thinking of his Jones family from the first in terms of the stage on which he must ultimately present them. And this does not mean that he falsifies them, although he might. What it does mean – and this is why he succeeds – is that he sees them as he intends the audience to see them. And he succeeds because he creates on the two levels on which his audience must respond.

On this second level of theatrical presentation, of stage technique and skills, contrivance and convention, you cannot have everything. If you are writing in verse, you cannot be writing in prose. If the characters are stockbrokers, they cannot behave and talk like troubadours. If the action must be fast, then it cannot at the same time be slow. Certain things cancel out other things. The point, made like this, seems so obvious that it does not seem worth making. Yet it is a fact that intelligent writers on the Theatre are always missing it. They are always asking dramatists for the impossible. They will not realise that every theatrical convention, all the work on this level we are discussing, has its particular virtues and defects, and that although the experienced dramatist will try to minimise the defects while exploiting the virtues, the limitations of the chosen form and style must be accepted.

Do you want an example? Here is one. Would you like a play in which the action tightly unwinds like a coiled spring and every single speech develops the situation, but a play, too, in which the characters are all created and exhibited in the round and are if anything larger than life? Yes, you would. So would I. And it can't be done, just because large characters in the round need plenty of space and plenty of time to display themselves, and this means a certain looseness of construction, which immediately rules out any tight economical handling, any action uncoiling like a spring. Take your choice, but do not ask for both at once.

We arrive at a greater confusion still, in which hardly anybody seems to know what he is talking about, when we come to consider the question of poetry in the Theatre. In my first talk I pointed out that this subject seems to exist in a permanent muddle here just because our greatest poet and our greatest dramatist happen to be one and the same man, Shakespeare. This encourages critics to tell us that all we need to do to save the Theatre, make it glorious again, is to bring back the poets. They find it convenient to forget that Yeats, to my mind the greatest poet writing in English of this century, spent a great deal of his time in the Theatre, was more intimately concerned with a Theatre than most poets will now ever find it possible to be, but these critics do not implore us to begin reviving the many plays that Yeats left us. They would be the first to point out their faults if we did. T S Eliot has made what seems to me a very gallant attempt to write contemporary poetic drama, not altogether without success, but clearly, to my mind, having to sacrifice too much, flattening his poetry and at the same time over-simplifying both character and action.

You cannot, you see, have everything. If, for example, you want the contemporary poet to retain his allusive and complex imagery and the intricacies of this thought and feeling – and it is for these he is celebrated and admired – then how is he to write dramatic dialogue that can be immediately understood by an audience? Again, one lively American critic has told us he wants poetic drama not only for its verbal splendour but also because it moves with a speed that plodding realistic prose drama cannot begin to achieve. But in fact it is only in certain situations, of great emotional intensity, that verse is the better dramatic medium; and at other times, dealing with situations that this critic would demand in a play about our own age, it tends to make very slow work, heavy weather indeed, of scenes that a prose realist would handle easily and economically. You can of course have the high spots in verse, and the ordinary scenes in realistic prose, but so far this blend of two very different conventions has not worked well.

I am not going to discuss the dramatist's technical problems here, for our final broadcast in this series will be itself a discussion programme, in which, I hope, the younger dramatists taking part will mention these problems. Here I prefer to make a final point that is in itself a sort of warning to listeners beginning to write plays. Just now our younger dramatic critics seem to be passionately concerned with a play's dialogue and with nothing else in it. They appear to believe that a heightened or unusual quality of dialogue is sufficient by itself, even though everything else in the piece is inferior or dubious, to lift a play into the highest class. I believe this to be wrong. I must confess I do not myself much admire some of the dialogue these critics praise so enthusiastically, notably that unpleasing mixture of excessive slangy violence with unreal, super-literary high-falutin found now in so many American plays. True, most of our English realistic plays contain a great deal of flat dialogue, but that is because the English life they present also contains a great deal of flat dialogue; and in this respect the English dramatist is much worse off than his Irish, American and French colleagues. The English hate making a scene; but the dramatist *has* to make a scene.

I will end now by warning young writers that although plays are written in dialogue, that dialogue must be spoken by characters of unusual quality too, and those characters must be involved in an action that seems to us significant and that, if possible and without obtrusive symbolism, makes us feel that it casts a long shadow. On one level a play must be satisfying strictly as a play, and on the other level it must be disturbing, stimulating, inspiring, as an image of life. In my next talk I shall discuss the relation between the dramatist and his fellow artists in the Theatre.

The Listener, 12 December 1957

The Dramatist and his Colleagues

In the 1890s Henry James tried hard to become a successful dramatist and failed rather disastrously. He wrote to his brother William:

> The whole odiousness of the thing lies in the connection between the drama and the theatre. The one so admirable in its interest and difficulty, the other loathsome in its condition...

Having spent more time working in the Theatre than Henry James did, I have often cursed it longer and louder than he did. I have declared over and over again, both in and out of print, that the whole organisation of the Theatre ought to be taken to pieces and then carefully put together again in a more sensible and civilised fashion. Of course the thing can be odious, loathsome, a dramatist's nightmare and heartbreak. But it is all the dramatist has to work with, to be a dramatist. Trying to take the drama away from the Theatre is like trying to take the symphony away from the orchestra and the concert hall. If there is no Theatre, there is no drama; and indeed no dramatist, only an author giving us something else to read. That is why I have little patience with what might be called the donnish or 'Eng Lit' attitude towards the drama, which tries to take the dramatist out of the Theatre where he belongs, and lock him up in a library.

It should be plain by now that the theory of the drama I have sketched in these talks – the idea that the drama exists to provide us with what I have called 'dramatic experience' brought about by our response on two different levels of the mind – places the dramatist squarely where he belongs, in the Theatre, if only because one of those essential levels accepts the fact that a play is being presented to us on a stage in a playhouse. This means that without the co-operation of his fellow workers in the Theatre – the directors, players, designers, and the rest – the dramatist cannot truly function as a dramatist. No Theatre, no drama. That is how it stands.

Holding these views then, I am the last man who would pretend, in order to glorify the dramatist, that the drama is not a co-operative and communal art. Indeed, my theory gives the actor more importance than most other theories do, though not more than playgoers themselves do, and they may be instinctively wiser in this matter than most theorists when they decide what playhouse to visit. According to my idea of dramatic experience, the audience is equally conscious of the character being played and the actor or actress who is playing that character. I believe this double response to be essential to the true experience. So, for example, if Peggy Ashcroft is playing Hedda Gabler, then we reject the true experience not only if we simply see Peggy Ashcroft and not Hedda Gabler – and that is obvious – but also, and this is not so obvious, if we only see Hedda Gabler and not Peggy Ashcroft. The genuine, unique experience, which gives the drama its own particular character and value, comes from Peggy-Ashcroft-playing-Hedda-Gabler, a real woman and an imaginary woman who for a space of two or three hours are magically transformed into one person, without either the actress or the character completely losing her identity. And this explains our attitude towards actors and acting. It is precisely those players who achieve this balance who attract us to the Theatre. It is the star performers above all others who are always tremendously themselves – an Ashcroft, an Edith Evans, an Olivier, a Richardson – and yet at the same time somebody else, the characters they are playing. For this is what the Theatre demands if it is to fulfil its peculiar function.

It cannot be said, then, that I am trying to reduce the stature of the actor, no matter how naturally prejudiced I may be in favour of the dramatist. Holding this theory, I feel I am not entitled even to resent the fact that it is generally the leading actor's or actress' name outside the playhouse and not the dramatist's that brings in the audience. This is inevitable and does no harm so long as certain things are remembered, not by playgoers, for it is not their concern at all, but by these leading players themselves. For there is always a danger that, acclaimed as they are, sought after as they are, knowing themselves to be the magnet that draws the public, they will begin to forget their essential dependence upon the dramatist.

That is why I am suspicious of any claims, popular with some critics, that at last the Theatre is being given back to the actors, that we are within sight of a return to the old actor-manager system. The danger here is that the actor, given supreme authority, begins to believe that the author exists not to challenge and inspire him with great parts but to provide him with what used to be called 'a vehicle', a play that would be nothing without him, a fat juicy part, conspicuous among a lot of thin dry little parts, a part that satisfies some vague or whimsical desire he happens to have – to appear as a cardinal, a detective, a blind musician, a prince of Ruritania. Again, the star actor's feeling of insecurity – and it is probably this feeling that decided him originally to be an actor, to complete himself on the stage, as somebody else not altogether himself – his fear of failure, which his public recognition only heightens, too often tempt him away from plays that are original, bold, challenging, and encourage him to decide on the safe second-rate, in which he hopes to repeat an earlier success. And because the right and rewarding relation between dramatist and player is not there, the audience gets a show but no true dramatic experience, with almost everything on the level of Theatre and little or nothing on the other level of a rich and vital imaginary life.

Although many people must co-operate to provide us with this experience, it must never be forgotten that the prime mover in the enterprise is the dramatist. To begin with, all the others have something to fasten upon; the dramatist has to conjure his play out of the empty air. There are now more and more people in the world, many of whom consider themselves far more important than authors and tend to be more and more richly rewarded, who cannot do anything until somebody else, sitting alone for weeks on end hard at work and not lolling in expensive restaurants over cigars and brandy, has created something for them to work on. The dramatist remains the original creator, the genuine magician plucking characters and scenes out of the empty air. And I declare emphatically that his pre-eminence is acknowledged whenever the Theatre is healthy and vital. Show me a theatre where the status of the author is low, and I will show you a bad theatre. And whenever a nation's Theatre has made history, you will find that it has had its own dramatists prominently associated with it.

Exciting theatres have always been writers' theatres. No matter how brilliant they may be, directors and actors are incapable of creating by their own efforts a theatre of the highest class, because such a theatre cannot rely entirely on revivals of old plays, it must produce important new work to be of the highest class, and that work must bring in the dramatist as the prime mover. And those theatres in which the author is merely an unhappy little man sneaking in and out of rehearsals, unregarded and forlorn, those theatres in which the dramatist's work is seen as so much rough raw material to be dyed and cut and trimmed to fit out a manager, director, or actor, even if it means turning tragedy into comedy, comedy into farce, are never never never theatres the world chooses to honour. They offer merchandise, not one of the arts, and the world knows it.

Young dramatists should be warned, however, that even when a theatre accepts them at their true value they will still have trouble. Dramatists, directors – or producers, if you like, though I prefer the American term director – and actors all depend upon one another, but like many other people who depend upon one another – the whole human race, for instance – they do not necessarily agree and all pull the same way. The dramatist does not regard the enterprise of stage production in the same way that the director and actors do. Some people might object to my lumping the director with the actors in this fashion, and would say that the director occupies a middle position between the dramatist and the actors. And to some extent this is true. Nevertheless, in their manner of approach to the whole enterprise the actors and their director come so close, and are both so distinctly removed from the dramatist, that it seems to me better to lump them together.

The fundamental difference, I think, is this: the dramatist cannot help feeling that his play already exists, and therefore all that the director and his actors have to do is to give it flesh and blood. The director and the actors may agree with this in theory, but in actual practice their whole approach is different. I think they really see themselves, first of all, as being pledged to produce between 120 and 150 minutes of entertainment for audiences who may have already started booking their seats, and this has to be done on the basis of this particular play that has been chosen. They start, you might say, from the opposite end. They do not believe that the play already exists, but only that in a few weeks' time, when they have done all they can for it, *a* play will come into existence. At the risk of being a bit too neat about it, we might say that director and actors begin with a general idea of theatrical performance, what should happen in a theatre, and end with this particular play, whereas the dramatist starts with the play, which seems to him already to exist, and ends within sight of a general idea of theatrical performance, what should happen in a theatre. The director and actors have to adjust their general idea to this play, while the dramatist has to adjust his play to the general idea. This is an exaggeration, as well as being a bit too neat, but does contain the truth about a complicated relationship.

Though they are all ready, if necessary, to make pretty first-night speeches about one another's work, each sees the evening, if it has been successful, as a triumph of his or her particular talent over difficulties contributed by the others. Secretly the dramatist believes that only about 75 or 80 per cent of his play has been offered to the public. The director and the actors, as soon as the author is out of hearing, congratulate one another on having made something worthwhile out of some tricky and rather dubious material: 'Look what we did to that tatty second act, old boy!' they say to one another. These differences of approach and outlook, together with some inevitable clashing of egos along the way, create a tension. But this tension, so long as it is not too great, thus making real co-operation impossible, is an aid rather than a hindrance to successful production, to the creation of dramatic experience for an audience. It helps, I feel, to give final shape, colour, tone and temper to what is being presented on the stage. Perhaps it explains why revivals rarely have the thrust and brilliance of first productions.

As the dramatist is the prime mover in the whole enterprise, his initial vision of what the audience ought finally to be shown should be deeply respected. Nevertheless, what he has imagined needs to be checked by what the directors and the players believe to be possible. And if the gap here is immensely wide, if the author's vision of what should be created is hopeless and impossible, then he is not in this instance functioning as a true dramatist. A true dramatist may – and indeed should – impose upon both his theatrical colleagues and his audiences his own original vision and idea of life, which may make their own peculiar demands on directors, players, designers, but these will always be possible demands, which the Theatre, if it is not too narrow and obstinate, can fulfil. Politics has been defined as the art of the possible. Well, theatrical production and indeed the drama itself have to be the art of the possible. It has always seemed to me a fatal weakness of the greatly gifted Gordon Craig that he has largely devoted himself to the impossible instead of the possible.

Let us now consider that colleague of the dramatist that you may still prefer to call the producer while I, for once following American fashion, call him the director. He is a very recent arrival in the Theatre. There are still plenty of Theatre people old enough to remember when plays were produced by the leading actor or the stage manager, perhaps with some assistance from the author. Now we must have a director, and some very successful directors, especially on Broadway, are these days the most important persons in the Theatre, having more power and influence than any dramatist or star player. I may be prejudiced but I cannot help regarding this state of affairs with some suspicion. It throws things off balance. I find it hard to believe that persons whom authors and players did without for centuries should be more import-ant than either. There is to my mind something unhealthy, hysterical, about a director-dominated Theatre, in which some Napoleon of the playhouse is entitled to use everybody and everything as mere means towards expressing his own wonderful personality, which he believes is all the audience cares about. The trouble is that a director is bound to feel insecure once he has risen above his sensible interpret-ative job, for after all he cannot write as well as the author or act as well as his best actors, and he is the Johnny-come-lately in the business, so that the more important he becomes the more he defies this feeling of insecurity by colouring and shaping everything, often daubing and distorting it, to assert and exhibit his personality.

This may result in brilliantly successful effects, as it has done during recent years on Broadway, creating a definite style of production and strongly influencing both authors and actors; but even in this style, it seems to me, there is something unbalanced, hysterical, violent, and neurotic. Too many of these successful and much-admired American productions are dedicated to nothing but a drama of nerves, in which the smallest disagreement between characters flares up at once into a shouting and screaming match, and the audience is always being brutally assaulted. It is 'good Theatre', as people say, but not very civilised drama.

But it is one thing to object, as I do, to the superman master-mind director, and quite another thing to doubt if directors are necessary at all. I have often been asked if dramatists should direct their own plays. I know several who do, and I have had to do it more than once myself, though never at my own request. There are several reasons why it is better to leave the production of your play to somebody else. In the first place, it is a good thing to bring another mind to a play; it is like lighting an object from a new angle, so obtaining a different view of its structure. And this mind will be fresher than the author's, so far as this play is concerned; and it can achieve a certain detachment impossible to the author. We authors are apt to fall in love with certain scenes, certain speeches, and sometimes these need to be modified, to be cut; but if we are the directors, then they will remain untouched. Finally, very few dramatists are as patient and tactful at handling players as an experienced director is; and they are apt, as I know I am, to become bored or irritated and impatient, hearing the speeches they have written, and lived with, spoken badly over and over again, or delivered simply as groups of words when the actors have only half-memorised them. And then the actors tend to be rather suspicious of an author's direction, for the reason I suggested earlier, that the author, unlike the director, does not belong to their camp, and his approach to the whole enterprise is different from theirs. So let us retain the director, without whom most actors now would feel lost, so long as he still feels himself to be the servant of the play as well as being the master of its production, so long as he remembers that he is not the essential creator, the prime mover; it is the dramatist.

Fashions in production, fashions in acting, change like fashions in clothes. During the 1930s, I remember, Granville Barker consented to come out of his retirement from the Theatre to direct a revival of one of his own plays. Many of us who were not old enough to have seen the original Granville Barker productions eagerly awaited the chance of seeing what this fabulous director could do. But – alas! – the production when it came seemed to most of us rather slow, ponderous, stilted. There had been a change of fashion, another convention was now in favour. In my first talk I said that while we had a right to our tastes and preferences, we must not believe that one convention alone, only one way of writing, producing, acting plays and one way alone, was capable of creating true dramatic experience. In the same way we must not believe, as some enthusiasts would have us believe, that a change of fashion in the Theatre is the Day of Judgement. Too much is argued from too little.

For example, disciples of the notorious 'method' in New York tell us that the player can act properly only out of his or her deeply-felt experience. It must all come, they tell us, from inside. So, if an actor has to play the part of a man waiting for a bus – to take a crude instance – then before he is ready to play it, he must go and wait for buses, saturate himself in bus-waiting. I disagree. The true actor is the man who can show you what it is like waiting for a bus without ever having had to wait for a bus himself. This is what makes him an actor. He can imagine himself into situations and then makes use of his ability to convey what he imagines. This is once again work on two different levels at the same time. It connects up with the dramatist's two levels, and those two levels on which the audience must ultimately respond.

The dramatic critic, too, must appreciate what is happening on each of these levels. This does not always happen. When *Look Back in Anger* first appeared at the Royal Court Theatre, most of the morning-newspaper critics said it was a poor play whereas most of the weekly-paper critics said it was a play of unusual quality. Discounting judgements that were merely personal and whimsical – and too much of our criticism now is little more than that – this wild discrepancy can be explained by the fact that each set of critics was favouring one of the two levels at the expense of the other. The daily-paper men, for the most part older men, were judging and condemning it on the level of theatrical construction, contrivance, effectiveness, tact; while the younger men on the weeklies were judging and praising it on the other level, on which they felt, rightly too, that new life was being brought to the Theatre.

In spite of a widespread legend that I am for ever doing battle with dramatic critics – though nobody ever explains how and where – I do not in fact look back in anger on them, having done the job myself once and knowing its difficulties. Many of them, I feel, have to see and report upon too many new productions, and go on too long without a break, with the result that either they become stale or wilful and capricious, like yawning oriental despots longing for new sensations. And all of them, both in London and New York, seem to me to take too little interest in the prevailing conditions of theatrical production. They write and behave as if the Theatre existed in an economic and social vacuum.

With writers of books on the drama, as distinct from the men who have to criticize new productions, I find I have on the whole less sympathy. As a rule they have spent too much time in the library and the lecture room and far from sufficient time actually in the Theatre, where the drama has its being, where dramatic experience is truly created. A play is not something to be read but something to be performed. Nobody can adequately criticise the work of the dramatist unless he or she is familiar with that work where it belongs, in the Theatre. And it seems to me absurd that towns can have courses of extension lectures on the drama when they do not even possess a theatre. Stop the lectures, I would say, and start a theatre. So, too, the drama should not be a subject at a university unless, like so many American universities, that university has its own theatre, a real theatre producing plays that audiences pay to see. Even if such a drama school should have courses in playwriting, about which I must admit I am not too hopeful, little harm will be done, and indeed much good might be done indirectly, so long as the theatre itself is just round the corner. We might enlarge that and say that there is no art of the drama or the dramatist unless the theatre itself is just round the corner. It may be one of half a dozen different kinds of theatres, all representing different theatrical conventions, but the players must be there in their playhouse: this is the body of which the immortal art of the drama is the soul.

The Listener, 19 December 1957

From the Discursive Notes to
The Art of the Dramatist

Dramatic Experience

As the father of five children and the grandfather of many more, I have had to do a great deal of clowning to entertain them. (Perhaps my success as a family entertainer partly explains why I have been able to keep many different kinds of audiences amused.) On these occasions, dramatic experience arrives at once. A small girl of five, eager and excited, eyes like lamps, demands that you turn yourself into some fantastic creature of your or her invention. You plunge into the impersonation. What happens? You notice at once a flicker of fear in her eyes as fat comfortable old Grandpa changes into this monster, and there is a note of uncertainty in her encouraging shriek. Overdo the performance at this point, and she backs away from you, might even burst into tears and run. So you make it plain that Grandpa is still there, trying to play the little game she wanted you to play, but keep the fantastic impersonation going too; and then, with any luck, she is happily divided, responds on both levels, and so enjoys true dramatic experience. And there is here, to my mind, the whole Theatre in miniature.

The last play I happened to see, before writing this [the original Old Vic lecture], was the Old Vic production of *Timon of Athens*, with Sir Ralph Richardson as Timon. It was divided into two acts, the first showing Timon as the princely host, the rich dupe, and ending with his disillusionment, the second displaying him as the misanthrope, the embittered hermit. Act One did not satisfy me because I was responding to it almost entirely on one level. I was not living with Timon; I was too conscious of Richardson's performance. There were special reasons for this: he and I are old friends who have done a good deal of work together in the Theatre; I saw at once that he was making the fullest possible use of certain mannerisms, pushing them to the brink of absurdity, in order to float his way through these early scenes, in which Timon is everybody's dupe, withdrawing most of his weight from the character, hardly identifying himself with it, making this act a mere preparation for the next, when he would discover for us the brooding, half-mad misanthrope. For this sketchy play, which Shakespeare probably roughed out in an ugly mood and then never troubled to complete, presents the leading actor, on whom all depends, with a very tricky problem. Timon is transformed so quickly and ruthlessly that if the actor fully creates and identifies himself with one Timon he is bound to fail in the other. If Timon in Athens captures our imagination, then Timon in exile will lose it, appearing merely an affected bore. Clearly, Richardson, by pushing these mannerisms at us, suggesting a man moving and speaking almost in a trance, had decided to sacrifice the Timon in part one to the Timon would who appear in part two, a sound theatrical conclusion. This explains why in Act One I was more conscious of Richardson's problem and of his possible solution of it than I was of Timon's situation in Athens, why my response was almost entirely on one level. And in Act Two true dramatic experience arrived, for during much of it Timon in his new situation and Richardson's performance, now wonderfully alive, were brought into focus. My mind responded on both levels, eagerly and excitedly, and a poorish play yielded dramatic experience of exceptional quality. But this keen satisfaction, rising to delight, could only have been produced by the response of both levels at once, for I have little or no instinctive sympathy with bankrupt tycoons gnawing roots in caves: it was Timon-in-exile plus Richardson's personality-and-technique that did the trick.

Realism on the English Stage

Unquestionably, the modern London Theatre owes almost everything, for good or ill, to three people – T W Robertson, the dramatist, and the Bancrofts, as actor-managers. Their combined success, first at the little Prince of Wales Theatre and then at the Haymarket, opened a new chapter in theatrical history. The plays Robertson wrote specially for the Bancrofts seemed at the time to be triumphs of naturalism; their enemies called them the 'Cup and Saucer School'. Short-winded staccato dialogue, still much used by Noël Coward and other writers of light comedy, makes its first appearance in Robertson's plays. It was Robertson, as producer of his own plays (though the term was unknown then), who first insisted upon every movement and piece of 'business' being carefully rehearsed, in the fashion we have followed ever since. Before then, leading players rehearsed in a perfunctory fashion, deliberately concealing from their fellow players what they intended to do on the opening night. (I remember seeing a foreign star rehearsing with a bewildered English company in this old style.) And it was from Robertson that his friend W S Gilbert, who often watched him at work, learnt his severe discipline as a producer. The careful preparation and the increasingly elaborate staging of these Robertson plays could only be undertaken by a management that no longer worked with a stock company and the repertory system (easily handled when your scenes consisted of backcloths and wings and the very minimum of furnishing), but financed, mounted and cast each play in the hope of obtaining a long run. It was the Bancrofts too, successfully playing Robertson, who put in a maximum number of comfortable stalls, cut the programme to start later and finish earlier, in general 'elevated and refined the tone of the Theatre' and brought it and themselves, so to speak, into society. From then on, ladies and gentlemen carefully entertained, at eight-thirty every evening *except Sunday*, other ladies and gentlemen. Although members of the lower classes might still cram themselves into the pit and pack the benches in the hot gallery, from now on the stalls paid for and called the tune. The Bancrofts were in, the Crummleses were out. Much that was artificial, absurd, under-rehearsed and over-played, disappeared for ever into the remoter provincial towns, but with it, I suspect, went a swaggering vagabond magic that this careful genteel Theatre could never recapture.

'It is interesting to recall,' writes Bancroft, 'the great surprise caused in those days by such simple realistic effects, until then unknown, as the dropping of the autumn leaves through-out the wood scene of the first act, and the driving snow each time the door was opened in the hut.' But this was showman-ship, not an attempt to persuade the audience they were not sitting in a theatre. After all, if these same people had been invited to visit Regent's Park specially to see autumn leaves or driving snow, they would have refused to go. What they enjoyed was sitting in the theatre and seeing the leaves falling, the snow effect when the door opened. Moreover, these plays of Robertson's, quite apart from any question of showmanship and giving the audience a surprise or two, really did demand solid box sets and realistic furnishing and plenty of props and effects, because their action did not take place on mysterious blasted heaths or the sea-coast of Bohemia but in scenes more or less familiar to the audience. They were not dramatic poems but prose pieces, as natural as Robertson could make them, of mid-Victorian sentiment, comedy, social satire. They had to be staged in this solid realistic fashion to be workable and effective at all. Sixty years later, Mr Basil Dean was producing Galsworthy with the same care for realistic detail, and he was quite right to do so, for the kind of play Galsworthy wrote demanded this treatment to be effective. If the play is in the realistic or naturalistic tradition, then the staging, the production, the acting, must remain within that tradition. A critic is entitled to declare that he is tired of this particular theatrical convention, though I think if he were scrupulously truthful he would have to admit he was really bored by having to sit through too many bad examples of it; but he must not try to pretend that somehow it does not belong to the Theatre, that on the stage you can put on a crown or wave a sword but must not pass a cup of tea or light a cigar.

No, it is not the carefully realistic stagers of realistic plays who have been at fault and have done harm to our Theatre. It is the Irvings and Trees and their like who are the villains of this piece. They deliberately confused two quite different conventions, and their bad influence is still lingering. We read to this day admiring references to the elaborate care Irving gave to his Shakespearean productions at the Lyceum, how he enlisted the aid of the Royal Academy and the Society of Antiquaries and the British Museum, all the experts on armour and weapons and historical costume. To do what? Not to present plays like Robertson's *Ours* or *Caste*, realistic pieces about a particular time and place, but to produce plays in another tradition altogether, dramatic poems that belong to no historical period and have no exact locale. To produce Shakespeare as if he were Robertson writing about the Crimean War, is a grave offence against the Theatre. It is taking the imagination out of the imaginative drama. It is turning King Lear and Macbeth and Hamlet into waxworks. By the time we have arrived at real sand for *The Tempest*, real water and gondolas for *The Merchant of Venice*, live rabbits scampering about in Shakespeare's dream forests, the ultimate imbecility has been reached. Two different conventions and traditions have clashed head-on. The Theatre has schizophrenia. And it is this idiocy, not honest realism working within its own convention, that ought to have been bundled out of the Theatre.

The Dramatist at Work

Some notes on the subject might be helpful. Of course I do not know what happens in the minds of other dramatists. I can attempt to describe only my own processes. Let us simply call the whole level representing the *life* to be brought into the Theatre, 'L'. Then the other level, belonging to the *Theatre*, we can call 'T'. I say [in my description of dramatic experience] that right from the first the dramatist must work on L and T at the same time. This could be misleading. Suppose we divide the whole creative process into three. In the first stage of it, you are playing around with the idea. (You may in fact have to do some genuine research, but you are still playing around with the idea.) And here there is a great deal more L than T. Next, in the second period, you begin planning the play, and now there is more T than L. Finally, you start writing the piece, and now with any luck you ought to work on a genuine L-plus-T basis, functioning on both levels at the same time. You are simultaneously aware of your characters as personages in the imaginary life you are presenting and as so many parts of various kinds played by actors and actresses in a certain setting. At least, this is what happens to me, and I refuse to believe that other dramatists are quite different.

There must be some difference, of course. For example, I know some dramatists who spend a great deal of time in the second or planning period, whereas in my case it is usually very brief and there have been occasions when it can be said hardly to have come into existence at all. That is, I have not been aware of it as a separate stage of the proceedings. What has happened in these instances is that the first playing-around-with-the-idea period has been unusually long and a good deal of T has come into it, of which T I have not always been conscious. But then the final stage, the writing, has in these instances been exceptionally swift and easy, because I have found the L-plus-T basis at once. When for some reason or other I have found myself with a mass of L stuff, with T absent, so that there has to be a deliberate switching over from L to T, the result has never been so happy. It is when there is a rapid movement between them, L becoming T, T becoming L, that one feels confident, even inspired. Let me give a concrete example, if only as a welcome relief from this suggestion of geometry and algebra. Many people, I have reason to know, were deeply moved by the final scene in *Johnson Over Jordan*. In this scene Johnson, the last of his happy memories having left him, is alone with the figure of Death, who removes the terrifying mask and shows a wise, kind face and tells Johnson it is time for him to go. So Johnson says goodbye to this world, this life, and, a small, lonely, but not ignoble figure, moves towards the vast unknown universe. Now every impressive T effect here – the stage emptying itself first of people and then of furnishings and warm light, the highly dramatic unmasking, the great bare stage, the sugges-tion of depth behind and then the glitter of stars, the slow walk of the actor, now wearing his bowler and carrying his little bag, as one instrument of the orchestra after another joins in the solemn music – was not something added to what had already been thought out on the L level; it arrived spontaneously at that point on L, was decisively what had to happen on the stage, and so the creation of this finale, for which there were detailed stage directions in the original script, was a successful example of L-plus-T. But remember, I am only claiming credit for my own share. The dramatic experience moving the actual audiences owed much to Mr Basil Dean's exceptional knowledge and resourcefulness, to the acting of Mr Richard Ainley as the masked figure and, above all, to Sir Ralph Richardson's wonderful Johnson. Here, however, we are concerned with the dramatist at work.

One member of my little 'seminar' at the Arts Council asked if it was advisable to write a play from a careful detailed synopsis. I replied that it was not my own practice and explained why. Synopses of this kind are generally written in cold blood, with what one might call the front of the mind applying itself to the task. My experience is that heat and pressure bring in other parts of the mind, set the imagination to work, put L and T into one focus. Therefore, the dramatist who does more than make use of a brief synopsis as a rough guide and reminder, who ties himself while actually writing to what has been coldly conceived by only part of himself, is not likely to achieve much inspired writing, any great imaginative strokes. And though plays ought to be tidily constructed (which is what the synopsis-man is aiming at) it is more important that they should be imaginative. Moreover, the imagination, the mind working at full pitch, can triumphantly solve technical problems that often baffle the cool planner, who is probably making laborious cross-references from L to T and T to L instead of compelling them to work together. Probably one reason why plays adapted from novels are rarely of high quality is that they can hardly ever be conceived on a true L-plus-T basis. The adapter finds all the L stuff given, and must then carefully add T to it; and this is far from being the L-plus-T I have described.

Another member of the 'seminar' seemed to think that my view of the creative process on two levels, as well as my later remarks about the dramatist's characters only existing in the scenes he has written for them, could be successfully challenged by a reference to the fact that Ibsen and other dramatists have made elaborate biographical notes about their characters. But when Ibsen is making these notes he is not writing a play; the creative process has not begun; he is busy in the first period, playing around with the idea, and at this stage it does not matter whether he merely broods over the characters or prefers to write their biographies.

Writing on a true L-plus-T basis, working on both levels at once, often enables one, among other things, to make a virtue out of a necessity. Here is a relatively simple instance. A woman arrives to stay, is carelessly or badly dressed, has not bothered about her appearance, looks unattractive. She goes off to change, and on her return looks a different creature, a dazzling charmer. A writer not functioning on the T level will probably be so eager to show what happens after the transformation that he will not allow the actress sufficient time to re-do her hair and face and change her clothes, even if she is using a quick-changing room in the wings. The old T hand will not make this mistake; he will probably earn the actress's gratitude by allowing her plenty of time; but while acknowledging the necessity he will probably not make a virtue of it, will not succeed in elaborating or strengthening the situation on the stage while the actress is off, changing. But if he is able to work with L-plus-T, it is more than likely that instead of keeping things merely ticking over while the actress is changing he will realise that he can use these ten minutes to make the scene of his re-entrance far more effective than it might have been. But 'realise' is probably misleading in these circumstances; it suggests – at least, to me – a problem spread out and reflected upon; but his mind will not be working in that fashion; he will probably have made a virtue out of this necessity without knowing he was doing it, one half of his mind timing the actress's change, the other half swiftly building up the scene during her absence.

Finally, what about writing parts for certain players? I am so far from being opposed to it that I consider the absence of this opportunity one of the weaknesses of the London Theatre, in which new plays are rarely performed by stock companies. Writing parts for certain players must not be confused with something quite different, namely, the old hack practice of providing, usually at their suggestion, actor-managers with 'vehicles'. Here the author does not write the play he wants to write but the one the actor-manager demands that he should write. He is doing not a creative but a catering job. But a man may be writing parts with certain players in mind, and creating a dramatic masterpiece. What was good enough for almost every great dramatist from Shakespeare to Chekhov (see his letters) is good enough for the rest of us. On the comparatively few occasions when I have been able to follow their example – for the improvised producing of the London Theatre makes it almost impossible – I have found it challenging, stimulating and finally rewarding. It helps, I have noticed, on both levels, even though it belongs itself entirely to T. But while I would be happy working with a stock company, it would have to be a large one (offering me, let us say, a choice of 30 players for ten characters), much larger, indeed, than the present economics of our Theatre would allow. Nevertheless, even on our commercial basis, with all its necessary economies, whenever a management has adopted a definite policy and has built up a company to interpret that policy, it has begun to achieve something instead of floundering around. Thus, the old Aldwych farces were no masterpieces of wit and humour, and the company, almost a stock company, that played them was not blazing with great talent, but these Aldwych productions had a pleasant and profitable place in the London life of the 1920s, are remembered with gratitude when hundreds of theatrical enterprises have been forgotten, just because a policy and a playhouse and an author and a company for once were closely and securely linked. Theatre work in any circumstances can hardly escape being difficult and precarious, but now we have made it ten times more difficult and precarious than it need be. Much of the energy and attention that ought to be given to the work is wasted now looking for and making sure of the work. The Theatre has sufficient problems of its own without our putting it at the end of an obstacle race.

Technique

Either there ought to be more of this stuff or less, probably none. I used to possess a big fat American book, which somebody must have borrowed and kept, that regarded play-writing as a sort of engineering job. There was a standard formula that applied to everything from *The Trojan Women* to *Getting Gertie's Garter*. This nonsense would do a young writer more harm than good. Others, like William Archer's *Play-Making*, Granville Barker's *Dramatic Method*, C K Munro's *Watching a Play*, could do little harm and might prove most useful.

How much can be taught? I don't know, never having been either teacher or pupil. Probably the chief value of a course like the famous one run by Baker at Harvard was not so much in the actual instruction as in the mutual criticism of the class itself, encouraging everybody to be highly conscious of dramatic problems. The creation of an elaborate mystique of play construction and theatrical technique is generally associated not with great imaginative dramatists but with second-rate men making the most of their inside knowledge and experience, the types who used to be 'play doctors'. On the other hand, I must confess I have always been surprised at the way in which so many clever writers, without theatrical experience, seem to lose all common sense when they try their hands at a play. The enterprise seems to go to their heads. They will submit, as a three-act play, a script that would not occupy the stage half-an-hour. They will introduce, for a scene lasting five minutes, a set that would take thirty men twenty minutes to erect. They will demand impossibilities of everybody. And when clever people can be as silly as this, I am certain it means that the Theatre is not for them; they are just not holding it in their minds at all. The people who will one day write good plays may at first make a number of minor technical mistakes, but as a rule they have the general feel of the thing, are in fact beginning to work simultaneously on the two levels.

Some personal notes may not be out of place here. I was very fond of the Theatre as a youth, and in my middle teens I even had thoughts of becoming an actor; but during the later period, nearly ten years, when I was writing for a living but had not begun to write plays, I cannot say I was specially devoted to the Theatre, was always attending it, reading and thinking about it. After the age of 17 I never had a 'stage-struck' period when everything about the Theatre fascinated me. And at no time since I turned dramatist have I ever led the life of the successful man of the Theatre – attending first nights, rushing round dressing-rooms, sending telegrams to everybody, exchanging gossip at late supper parties, generally behaving like a young actress who has made his first hit. When for the time-being I have finished working in the Theatre, I want to get away from it, to be out of its atmosphere. Its famous 'glamour' worked best for me about 1911, when I used to queue outside the gallery door of the Theatre Royal, Bradford, and watch, with wonder and joy touched with envy, the actors on their way to the stage door, with their trilbies perched on their brilliantined curls, their outrageous overcoats barely clearing the ground, fabulous beings far removed from the wool trade. It was then and there, and never again, I took my portion of honeydew and the milk of paradise. The Theatre to which I went to work, 20 years later, was something quite different.

My first job, for which I had had no real preparation, was to collaborate with Edward Knoblock in dramatising my novel *The Good Companions*. Knoblock had done a lot of this work; he was the 'play doctor' type. From him I learnt a number of useful technical points – to delay an entrance here, to hurry an exit there, and so forth – but I made a discovery that was more important. We had a scene at the end – I think it was my idea originally but will not swear to it – showing Oakroyd boarding the liner that would take him to his daughter in Canada, so fulfilling his heart's desire. And for this short scene I refused to write any dialogue. What with the liner hooting, our orchestra playing, the audience cheering and clapping, I argued, no dialogue could be heard. And if the scene was not as uproarious as that, if it needed dialogue, then it should not be there at all. Knoblock did not agree, and when I still persisted, he appealed to our manager and producer, Julian Wylie, who strongly supported him. They were old hands, I was a new boy, I must be reasonable, and so forth. But I would not give in: for once I knew in my bones I was right and they were wrong. So, with much shaking of older and wiser heads, the scene went in exactly as I wanted it, with not a word of dialogue. And what happened was exactly what I had told them would happen: the liner hooted, the orchestra played, the audience cheered and clapped, a little man walked up a gangway into a big ship. I decided then that at times, when my imagination was hard at work, when I felt excited about what I was doing, I might have an instinct, an insight, an intuition, worth more than years of experience and a knowledge of all the technical tricks.

So I wrote, at great speed after much brooding over the subject, a play called *Dangerous Corner*, which the daily paper critics did not like. Neither did Knoblock, for I remember running into him, at the back of the circle, on the second or third night, and he was tittering away at my confused attempt to work independently, without his experience and knowledge of what to do and what not to do, and hardly bothered to hide his derision when he caught sight of me. (This suggests he was an unpleasant fellow, which in general he was not; indeed, he was courteous, amiable, helpful; but there was in him a certain feline malice that the Theatre, a notably successful tempter, brought out and sharpened.) But the play, by no means my own favourite, has been running somewhere ever since, literally from the Arctic to the Amazon, so I could have had, if I had wanted it, the last titter. Perhaps Knoblock's odd behaviour that night – for he was neither stupid nor ill-mannered – was really defensive; he was an old-fashioned technician, whose Theatre was fast going; so his tittering was a kind of whistling in the dark.

As I write this, I have behind me quarter of a century's work in the Theatre, and there are few tricks of the trade I do not know. With what result? I have to plan and plot far more carefully than I did 20 years ago; I write at about half the speed; I have to re-write whole scenes where once I might not have changed a hundred words in a complete script; and even then I commit blunders and fall into traps I would have once avoided with ease. And this has nothing to do with any general loss of energy and failure of ability: it applies only to my playwriting. With all this experience and technical knowledge supporting me, it takes me far longer to write a play, and I do it with far more sense of difficulty than I used to do when I lacked this experience and knowledge. The reason, I suggest, is this: that for various reasons I no longer have the deep emotional drive towards creation in the Theatre that I had once, and that without this terrific impetus I find it far more difficult to work quickly and surely on both those necessary levels at once. This simultaneous working demands a greater release of energy than my present attitude towards the Theatre is likely to bring me. Do not mistake me: I am not crying stinking fish! The plays are all right when I have finished them. But all my experience and all the technical skill I have acquired down the years bring me less – even on their own level – than was once magically bestowed upon me by my desire to conquer the Theatre.

If I were addressing a class of young writers of prose drama, I would say to them: Above all, try to avoid a constant dribble of not very important speech, like conversation at a dinner party. It is this more than anything else that makes intelligent people think our prose drama so banal and boring. Don't behave towards the audience as if you were a polite hostess and felt compelled to keep going some sort of dialogue. As long as it is obvious your characters are up to something, allow them at times to be silent or at least laconic. And if they are not feeling very much, then severely ration their words. But then, when they are carried away by emotion, let them be eloquent, give them a fat juicy thumping good speech, as rich as the character can stand. More silent actions, more terse bare speeches cut to the bone, more sudden explosions into eloquence – yes, more of all these, and less and less and less of semi-polite, semi-explanatory talk, neither terse nor eloquent, stuff not coming from the brain nor from the heart but from social conscientiousness, party talk. But don't imagine if you can work this, you have a play. You still need people, and people involved in a significant action. But given the people, given the significant action, this method of handling dialogue will rid you of that woolly, bumbling, buzzy effect, that conventional dinner-party atmosphere, which is what most of our critics are really complaining about. It is the absence of this effect, this atmosphere, in the work of the best Americans that encourages these critics to over-praise them. What they don't spot in this American work, either because they don't want to or because their ears aren't good enough, are the false notes of violence-at-all-costs and cheap-slang-suddenly-turning-into-self-conscious-fine-writing. Also, they don't know how much harder it is for us mumbling, hate-a-scene-old-boy English to write exciting realistic plays about ourselves. However, that is our problem, not theirs. Class dismissed!

1957

METHODS AND ADVICE

THE DEMAND for actable plays – not great plays or even fine plays, but just actable ones – is undoubtedly much greater than the supply. One management alone, known to me, has read over 200 new scripts during the last eight months, and among them has not found half-a-dozen that seemed worth serious consideration. It is always possible of course that a work of original genius has been dismissed by a playreader, but it is my own experience that the ordinary run of scripts submitted is of very low quality.

The commonest fault is sheer lack of elementary theatrical technique, mostly the result of a failure to study the conditions of play producing and acting. Even intelligent experienced writers, novelists and critics, will offer play scripts that contain appalling blunders, asking for impossible effects, monstrous scene changes, and the like. Often they write as if they had never been inside a theatre or as if there were no difference technically between a play and a film. Where there are no obvious technical deficiencies, the commonest fault, especially among Theatre people themselves, is serving up the same old mixture of the same old stuff, with tea and cocktails at all hours in the Surrey lounge hall, comic butlers, pert maids, amorous couples drearily trying to sort themselves out by bedtime. More serious types usually offer the good old family chronicle play (with Munich on the wireless in the second act), with the seniors always wrong and the juniors always right – and Left. There is an obvious lack of new backgrounds – for example, a steel mill, a shoe shop, a short-wave therapy clinic, a vestry, a mayor's parlour, a Labour Exchange, an old oak tearoom, a West African brothel, an Australian fortune-teller's back parlour. And here is a tip: if you cannot mix people up in a new way (and this is hard to do), then mix them up in the old way but in some astonishing new settings.

And here is another tip – for the more advanced practitioners. If your treatment is strange and experimental, then keep your characters and their relationships fairly conventional and easily recognized. But if the characters and their relationships are odd and original, then make your dramatic treatment of them straightforward and conventional. If all is wild and original, the audience will be baffled. If all is conventional, the audience will be bored. And you cannot write plays successfully without the willing co-operation of the audience.

from 'With and Without Prejudice, Playwriting',
The Author, Spring 1948

I dislike beginning and I often spend a long time pondering over a play or a novel (although I make few notes) before starting to write. Once I have begun, however, I work regularly, usually every morning and early evening, and generally with considerable concentration and speed. Odd bits of work, such as short essays and articles, I may do at odd times. Having been typing now for well over 30 years, I work directly on to a typewriter, and in fact cannot use a pen except for short corrections. For real creative work of any length I must have complete seclusion, although in my time I have done quite a lot of work in hotel bedrooms, trains, theatres, ships, radio offices and studios. Once I have made a start – and it is the act of beginning that demands a certain amount of 'inspiration' – I often work better if publishers and theatres managers are anxiously demanding results from me; and unlike many playwrights and novelists I rarely work far ahead of possible production or publication. One rule of mine, which I commend to younger authors, is never write on the spot – for example, I wrote about London in Arizona, and about Arizona in London. I began writing very early in life – it is 40 years since I sold my first article to a London paper – and would seem to have been destined for a literary career; but I picked a bad time for it and, if I could have my life over again, I do not think I would choose to be an author.

The Author, c 1951

My usual method with a play is to jot down a few notes in a notebook and then to do nothing about them for a long time. Sometimes I never do anything about them at all. With ideas in notebooks it's a question of the survival of the fittest. Then, I suddenly feel impelled to write the play, and begin thinking about it really hard.

The actual process of writing doesn't take me long. What people call my serious plays, *Dangerous Corner*, *Time and the Conways*, *An Inspector Calls* and *The Linden Tree*, were all written in about ten days. Yet some of my comedies, which I'm supposed to have dashed off in a moment of absent-mindedness, have taken me weeks and weeks to get right.

When I was younger I never used more than one draft of a play. After the first draft it wouldn't be necessary to change more than fifty words. Now I'm older and I find that I have to revise much more. It's a question of energy. One loses a certain drive...

Unlike some of the younger playwrights, my own primary interest in writing plays is the problem of their construction. The absence of good construction in so many of our newer plays worries me. Some of our writers have the feeling for the surface of a play, for dialogue, but to me there's a lot more to a play than that...solid architectural construction.

One's interest in characterisation changes, of course. When you are young you are fascinated by the infinite variety of human beings around you. Later you find that you become more interested in man as such and in his relation to the universe.

Books and Art, March 1958

He went into greater detail about his methods, relating them to particular plays, and spoke of his experiments, in a discussion on the radio; I have edited his part of the conversation.

A good dramatist has to work on two different levels of his mind more or less at the same time. This is the chief reason why it is hard to be a good dramatist. There are other reasons. You must be sensitive, but you must also work in the Theatre, which demands that you should be tough. So you must be tough and sensitive at the same time. The two different levels of the mind might be called the warm – imaginative – creative – deep level, and the cold – crafty – technical – upper level. A good play needs both.

In a play you are creating characters and atmosphere, a piece of life in which everything has significance, and you must do that from the deep level. Otherwise everything will be rather false, thin, characters cut out of cardboard, stagey rubbish. But you are also writing a piece for certain kinds of actors in a certain theatre. You may actually, as Chekhov did, be writing for one set of players in a definite theatre. And you must know that you have a stage of more or less certain size to work on, and that there will be present an audience with its own particular limitations. This is the technical job, done with the cool front of the mind; crafty planning.

All theatrical technique is a convention. I want to stress this point, because audiences and even many critics imagine that the convention they are familiar with is natural and right. Some people think any attempt to change the convention is a departure from good sense. But it's all convention. Naturalism – that is, the attempt to give a play the surface appearance of actual life – is itself only another convention. And it's essential that the convention should be changed, because after a time a technique becomes threadbare. When the notes on an instrument become too well known, you have got to increase the range and flexibility of the instrument, as Chekhov, for example, did.

I was known as a novelist, and it's always assumed that novelists must write large, untidy plays. So in *Dangerous Corner*, my first serious play, I deliberately concentrated on the 'Theatre', the technique. I wrote a very neat play, full of tricks and ingenuity, just to get my hand in. But it wasn't what I was really after. What I wanted to do was to bring to the stage something of the richness and the depth you get in a decent novel. Most plays seem so thin. I tried to do this in *Eden End*, which is, I think, actually a well-contrived play, but has the necessary richness and depth (I hope) so that nobody notices the contrivance. What I was chiefly after in *Eden End* was a sense of pathos first suggested by irony. I put back the time to 1912, before the last war, and that started dramatic irony at once.

I happened also to be interested in the metaphysical problem of Time itself, as well as in such effects as I could secure by moving plays about in time. I decided to turn this metaphysical interest to account in two plays. The first of these was *Time and the Conways*. In the second act I put the action forward 20 years, showing it in terms of a sudden vision of the future on the part of the chief character Kay Conway. Then, in Act Three, we returned to the point where we left off in Act One, with Kay at her birthday party in 1919. So the whole of Act Three should be haunted by the knowledge of Act Two. And Kay's obscure sense of it breaks through before the end.

In the second of these time plays, *I Have Been Here Before*, the whole time problem is more complicated. It depends on the theory that we live our lives over and over again with some differences. And the play doesn't depend on whether you believe it. It's fairly straightforward in construction. What specially interested me in it, apart from the really appalling difficulties in so small and tight an action, was the way in which I found it possible to cheat the audience gradually away from ordinary very realistic speech to deliberately heightened speech, without anybody noticing the shift.

In my next two plays I gave experiment its head. And because the method was to be so unusual, I kept the material fairly commonplace – in both *Johnson Over Jordan* and *Music at Night*: Johnson being deliberately ordinary in himself and his surroundings, and the characters in *Music at Night* being very familiar types. What I was chiefly after in both these plays was to take my characters out of ordinary time – as, of course, you might do in a dream play – and try to present them four-dimensionally, so to speak. In Act Three Johnson is doing something more than remembering his past. What he is really doing is moving freely in and out of the past, and re-creating the experiences he finds there, as we sometimes do in dreams. In these scenes, unless the audience realises that Johnson is playing a complicated double part, that he's back in the past and yet fundamentally out of time altogether, they will miss any force and depth these scenes may have. It's rather like getting a stereoscope into proper focus. And this explains, to my mind, why people differ wildly in their appreciation of these experimental plays – one set saying they are dreary and muddled, the other set declaring that they are a new and vital experience in the Theatre. For example, when Johnson in Act Three suddenly sees his children at the window, he is back again at some moment of time when they were all having a holiday together, and the children did appear at a window and talk to him, but he is also the man who is now out of time altogether, who tells his children what he always wanted to tell them, and never did, and so forth. This method, if it is successfully pursued, ought to bring what we see and hear on the stage very close to our own interior and secret life, to those dreams of ours so strange, moving, and oddly significant that they can make the day of waking life that follows them often seem flat and colourless.

The method makes enormous demands on director and actors, who must play with great flexibility and subtlety. And it needs the active co-operation of the audience. They must bring something more than their usual rather lazy curiosity. They must keep hold of the silken thread runing through the labyrinth.

The odd thing is that critics are often less capable of making this new response than ordinary fairly intelligent members of the public.

I used the same four-dimensional, in-and-out-of-time dream technique, for suggesting the secret inner life in *Music at Night*. In this I tried to dramatise the minds of a group of people who were listening to a new piece of music. In Act Two, for instance, which corresponded to the Adagio movement of the concerto, I assumed that the music released painful memories, fear and shame, and much that may have been repressed in the listeners' minds. I dramatised this release in a series of short scenes allotted to the various characters.

I'm afraid it went beyond the limits of the Theatre altogether. I wanted to suggest something that seems impossible to suggest on the stage, no matter what method you adopt, and that is the idea that personality is an illusion, a kind of mask.

And that is what is wrong with *Music at Night*, which has in it some of the best writing I have done for the stage.

'Curtain Up, The Playwright's Problem',
The Listener, 27 March 1941

There is a...quite unusual demand for...various kinds of plays, and I will deal with them briefly in turn. First, then, West End managers need new plays of quality for both London runs and provincial tours. These plays should be workmanlike and should also try to bring some new life into the Theatre. Too many of our plays are written by theatrical hacks who know all the old tricks and nothing else. They write about the same old stuff in the same old way. At the other extreme are writers who bring excellent new material but do not understand how to shape it properly. Such writers, who probably have the root of the matter in them, should turn themselves coolly into craftsmen.

The best way to discover faults in a play is to see it on the stage. Therefore, new dramatists with little practical experience would be well advised to persuade the nearest Repertory Theatre or decent amateur group to try their pieces out for them. You learn more this way than by sending manuscripts to Shaftesbury Avenue or to star players. Incidentally, actors and actresses are mostly very bad judges of plays in manuscript – for they read them in terms of the parts they fancy for themselves – though they are frequently excellent judges of actual productions. Have the play tried out, then, before posting it off to the West End.

This brings me to the next demand. The Repertory Companies need new plays too, and especially plays that do not give them too much trouble in the matters of cast, sets and costumes. Do not expect the Coketown Players to be excited about your terrific drama of Cavaliers and Roundheads, which needs eight huge sets, a cast of 30, and more clothes coupons than all Coketown has seen this year. In fact, just forget about this terrific drama. But the same people might jump at a new play, preferably fairly topical in interest, that demanded only one or two simple sets, a cast of six, eight or ten players, and some ordinary clothes. Moreover, if you are ambitious and can take long views, let me assure you that it is much better practice to try to grapple with these fairly simple theatrical conditions than it is to write grandiloquent and extravagant pieces that assume we already have a huge National Theatre.

But it is possible to be simpler still. And now we come to a very urgent demand indeed, and that is for effective new plays or playlets – they can be one, two or three acts long – that ask as little as possible from the producer, need only a few players, and have the minimum requirements in sets, costumes, lighting.

[...]

Nor is the writing of such unpretentious plays and playlets to be depised on other grounds. If you need money, they will soon earn some for you, and probably sooner than the unplayed masterpiece of yours now going the rounds in manuscript. You can see your work being performed before friendly but frank and critical audiences, and thereby learn a great deal. In fact, I know of no better way for a newcomer to dramatic writing to learn his or her job than this. And if there are any performances of this kind in your neighbourhood, try to attend a few of them – to note the limitations of productions and to observe typical audiences – before venturing into the field yourself.

[...]

Finally, whether you do a playlet for three people and a corner of a village hall or create a drama that requires the combined casts of *Love for Love* and *Heartbreak House*, you can express a vitally democratic and progressive point of view that will do everybody concerned a bit of good. But – and this is the point – set about it carefully. Stir the stuff well into the mixture before cooking. Don't hurl in it, at the last minute, great half-baked dollops of political propaganda that might have been found under the platform after the last Left Wing meeting. If you want your piece to have a social-political slant, shape your whole drama in these terms, and do not try to do it by compelling your characters merely to argue about these social-political matters. Shaw can do it this way, simply because he is the great dramatist-debater of our – and perhaps any other – time; but unless you bear in mind that you are not Shaw, you will come to grief. Also, unless you have a natural sense of humour, don't try to be funny, for the result is always painful. You can sometimes bluff the serious parts, but jokes have to be jokes, and if there is any doubt about them, leave them out. Humour is not essential. Eugene O'Neill was awarded the Nobel Prize.

Now, what do you do with these plays when you have written them? If you must, send them, with pre-paid return postage and adequate packing, to West End managers and to your favourite stars. But if you are sensible, you will send them to the producer at the nearest Repertory Theatre.

'Plain Words about Plays', *Tribune*, 10 September 1943

18th November, 1938.

Dear Mr. Berry,

There are three ways of getting your plays
on in London. The first is to persuade one of the
suburban repertory or "shop window" theatres to do
your play, and managers will always go to see plays where
they won't read them. The second method is to work
through a good energetic agent who will see to it that
when you have written the right play some manager takes
notice of that play. The third method, if you have
a play with a star part in it, is to persuade the
particular star you have in mind to read the play and
then he or she will probably be able to get it put on.
It is a fact that although a great many plays are sent
to them most star actors and actresses are short of suitable
plays. In addition I would add that it is much better to
see your plays played by anybody, a repertory company or
even a bunch of local amateurs, than not to have them
played at all. You learn a great deal by watching actual
performances of your play and while it is being done it is
much more a living thing than while it is still in manuscript

And please remember that at twenty-two your life
is by no means over. When my first play was produced in
the West End I was thirty-seven.

Yours sincerely,

Mr. Arthur R. Berry.